NORTH AMERICAN WETLANDS CONSERVATION ACT PROGRESS REPORT 2002~2003

North American Wetlands Conservation Council
January 2004

Table of Contents

North American Wetlands Conservation Act
Reporting Requirements

This document fulfills the requirements of Section 10 and 16 of the North American Wetlands Conservation Act of 1989.

Sec. 10. REPORT TO CONGRESS.
The Secretary shall report to the appropriate Committees on the implementation of this Act. The report shall include—

> (1) a biennial assessment of—
>> (A) the estimated number of acres of wetlands and habitat for waterfowl and other migratory birds that were restored, protected, or enhanced during such two-year period by Federal, State, and local agencies and other entities in the United States, Canada, and Mexico;
>> (B) trends in the populations size and distribution of North American migratory birds;
>> (C) the status of efforts to establish agreements with nations in the western hemisphere pursuant to section 16; and
>> (D) wetlands conservation projects funded under this Act, listed and identified by type, conservation mechanism (such as acquisition, easement, or lease), location, and duration.
>
> (2) an annual assessment of the status of wetlands conservation projects, including an accounting of expenditures by Federal, State, and other United States entities, and expenditures by Canadian and Mexican sources to carry out these projects.

Sec. 16. OTHER AGREEMENTS.

> (a) The Secretary shall undertake with the appropriate officials of nations in the western hemisphere to establish agreements, modeled after the (North American Waterfowl Management) Plan or the (Tripartite) Agreement, for the protection of migratory birds identified in section 13(a)(5) of the Fish and Wildlife Conservation Act of 1980 (16 U.S.C. 2912(a)). When any such agreements are reached, the Secretary shall make recommendations to the appropriate Committees on legislation necessary to implement the agreements.

Abbreviations Used in Tables

U.S. States/Territories

AK	Alaska
AL	Alabama
AR	Arkansas
AZ	Arizona
CA	California
CO	Colorado
CT	Connecticut
DE	Delaware
FL	Florida
GA	Georgia
HI	Hawaii
IA	Iowa
ID	Idaho
IL	Illinois
IN	Indiana
KS	Kansas
KY	Kentucky
LA	Louisiana
MA	Massachusetts
MD	Maryland
ME	Maine
MI	Michigan
MN	Minnesota
MO	Missouri
MS	Mississippi
MT	Montana
NC	North Carolina
ND	North Dakota
NE	Nebraska
NH	New Hampshire
NJ	New Jersey
NM	New Mexico
NV	Nevada
NY	New York
OH	Ohio
OR	Oregon
PA	Pennsylvania
RI	Rhode Island
SC	South Carolina
SD	South Dakota
TN	Tennessee
TX	Texas
UT	Utah
VA	Virginia
VT	Vermont
WA	Washington
WV	West Virginia
WI	Wisconsin
WY	Wyoming

Mexican States

BCN	Baja California Norte
BCS	Baja California Sur
CHIH	Chihuahua
CHIS	Chiapas
COAH	Coahuila
DF	Distrito Federal
DGO	Durango
GRO	Guerrero
GTO	Guanajuato
NAY	Nayarit
NL	Nuevo Leon
OAX	Oaxaca
QROO	Quintana Roo
SIN	Sinaloa
SON	Sonora
TAB	Tabasco
TAMPS	Tamaulipas
VER	Veracruz
YUC	Yucatan
ZAC	Zacatecas

Canadian Provinces

AB	Alberta
BC	British Columbia
MB	Manitoba
NB	New Brunswick
NF	Newfoundland
NS	Nova Scotia
NT	Northwest Territories
NU	Nunavut
ON	Ontario
PEI	Prince Edward Island
QC	Quebec
SK	Saskatchewan
YT	Yukon Territories

Project Type

A	Acquired
R	Restored
E	Enhanced
O	Other

Other

<10	Less than 10
NWR	National Wildlife Refuge
USFWS	U. S. Fish and Wildlife Service
WMA	Wildlife Management Area
WPA	Waterfowl Production Area

U.S. North American Wetlands Conservation Act Projects Arrayed by State
Acres Protected, Restored, and Enhanced in Fiscal Years 2002-2003
[Section 10(1)(A)]

Project Title	State	Acquired Acres	Restored Acres	Enhanced Acres	Date Approved
Agulowak River Protection Project	AK	80	0	0	6/20/2001
Izembek NWR Complex I	AK	21,565	0	0	9/21/2001
Izembek NWR Complex II	AK	21,781	0	0	3/19/2003
Spuhn Island Protection Project	AK	157	0	0	6/12/2002
Total		**43,583**	**0**	**0**	
Mobile - Tensaw Delta III	AL	12,682	405	0	3/14/2002
Total		**12,682**	**405**	**0**	
Arkansas Ecoregional Portfolio Sites I	AR	7,271	7,839	120	9/10/2002
Choctaw Island	AR	8,300	303	0	9/21/2001
Lower Mississippi Valley Ecosystem III	AR, LA, MS	2,778	11,278	31,617	9/21/2001
Total		**18,349**	**19,420**	**31,737**	
Southwest Wildlife Riparian Habitat Protection	AZ	60	60	60	6/20/2001
Total		**60**	**60**	**60**	
Bahia Acquisition	CA	639	0	0	9/10/2002
Butte Basin & Colusa Trough Wetland Habitat II	CA	0	295	30,822	9/10/2002
Jacoby Creek Easement Acquisition	CA	6	6	0	6/20/2001
Lakeview Farms Wetlands Conservation Project	CA	138	138	0	6/12/2002
Poso Creek Flood Plain Wetland Habitat Project	CA	3,510	6,714	5,773	3/14/2002
Simmons Slough Wildlife Corridor Acquisition Parcel #1	CA	70	0	0	6/20/2001
Yolo & Delta Basins Wetlands Restoration & Enhancement	CA	0	550	3,191	3/19/2003
Yolo Basin Wetland Habitat Project I	CA	7,694	875	4,618	3/19/2003
Total		**12,057**	**8,578**	**44,404**	
San Luis Valley Wetland Restoration Project II	CO	5,206	1,640	810	3/19/2003
South Park Valley Premier Wetlands & Mountain Plover Habitat	CO	10,959	1,880	0	3/14/2002
Total		**16,165**	**3,520**	**810**	
Inland Marsh Restoration in Natchaug State Forest	CT	0	55	0	6/12/2002
Total		**0**	**55**	**0**	
Chesapeake Bay Initiative II	DE, MD, PA, VA, WV	0	9,811	0	6/12/2002
Chesapeake Bay Initiative III	DE, MD, PA, VA, WV	0	17,400	0	9/10/2002
Delaware Coastal Plain Restoration Project	DE	0	46	0	6/20/2001
North Delaware Wetlands Rehab Program - Old Wilmington Marsh	DE	202	190	202	9/21/2001
Total		**202**	**27,447**	**202**	

Multistate projects are listed in each state where they occur. Full figures are given with each listing.

U.S. North American Wetlands Conservation Act Projects Arrayed by State
Acres Protected, Restored, and Enhanced in Fiscal Years 2002-2003
[Section 10(1)(A)]

Project Title	State	Acquired Acres	Restored Acres	Enhanced Acres	Date Approved
Burnett Lake Phase - San Felasco Conservation Corridor	FL	30	310	0	6/12/2002
Hammock Point Marsh Restoration at Tomoka State Park	FL	0	96	0	6/20/2001
Historic Cypress Forest/Swamp Restoration	FL	0	400	0	6/20/2001
Total		**30**	**806**	**0**	
Broxton Rocks Expansion Acquisition Project	GA	785	0	0	6/20/2001
Chickasawhatchee Swamp Habitat Conservation	GA	19,700	0	0	3/14/2002
Youmans Bird Pond Causeway Restoration	GA	0	31	0	6/12/2002
Total		**20,485**	**31**	**0**	
Hamakua Marsh Ecosystem Restoration & Community Development	HI	0	23	0	6/20/2001
Hawaii Wetlands - Oahu	HI	4,816	1,139	192	9/10/2002
Na Pohaku O Hauwahine Wetland Restoration In Kawai Nui Marsh	HI	0	1	0	6/20/2001
Total		**4,816**	**1,163**	**192**	
Iowa Glaciated Wetlands Initiative	IA	2,783	6	0	9/21/2001
Iowa Prairie Pothole Wetland Development Project	IA	0	0	117	6/12/2002
Middle Missouri River I	IA, NE	4,084	30	456	3/19/2003
Southern Tallgrass Prairie Wetlands Initiative	IA, MN	1,467	1,393	0	9/10/2002
Total		**8,334**	**1,429**	**573**	
Henry's Fork Wetlands	ID	869	2,002	0	3/19/2003
Teton River Basin Wetlands Conservation III	ID, WY	1,827	2,663	0	9/10/2002
Total		**2,696**	**4,665**	**0**	
Lower Kaskaskia River Wetland Restoration	IL	0	94	0	6/12/2002
Midewin Dolomitic Wetland & Prairie Restoration	IL	0	300	0	6/12/2002
Nygren Riparian Wetland Restoration	IL	0	590	0	6/20/2001
Rollins Savanna Wetland Restoration Project	IL	0	772	0	6/12/2002
Total		**0**	**1,756**	**0**	
Aboite Wetland Restoration	IN	97	0	0	6/20/2001
Total		**97**	**0**	**0**	
McPherson Valley Wetlands IV	KS	1,295	318	115	9/21/2001
Total		**1,295**	**318**	**115**	
Green River State Forest	KY	1,980	420	140	3/14/2002
Total		**1,980**	**420**	**140**	

Multistate projects are listed in each state where they occur. Full figures are given with each listing.

U.S. North American Wetlands Conservation Act Projects Arrayed by State
Acres Protected, Restored, and Enhanced in Fiscal Years 2002-2003
[Section 10(1)(A)]

Project Title	State	Acquired Acres	Restored Acres	Enhanced Acres	Date Approved
Acadiana Park Wetland Preservation	LA	130	0	0	6/12/2002
Chenier Plain Coastal Wetlands Restoration	LA	0	29,237	29,180	3/14/2002
Louisiana Coastal Wetlands II	LA	0	1,653	19,135	3/19/2003
Lower Mississippi Valley Ecosystem III	LA, AR, MS	2,778	11,278	31,617	9/21/2001
Pointe - Aux - Chenes Hydrologic Restoration	LA	14,54	4,736	1,224	3/19/2003
Total		**4362**	**46,904**	**81156**	
Nulands Neck Acquisition	MA	0	110	0	6/12/2002
O'Keefe Acquisition	MA	25	0	0	6/20/2001
Salt Marsh Restoration & Enhancement - Plum Island Sound - Great Marsh	MA	0	50	0	6/12/2002
The Ganson Trust Lands	MA	215	0	0	6/12/2002
Total		**240**	**160**	**0**	
Chesapeake Bay Initiative II	MD, DE, PA, VA, WV	0	9,811	0	6/12/2002
Chesapeake Bay Initiative III	MD, DE, PA, VA, WV	0	17,400	0	9/10/2002
Dividing Creek	MD	5,245	180	100	9/10/2002
Heart of the Chesapeake I	MD	19,318	125	0	9/21/2001
Heart of the Chesapeake II	MD	19,359	60	0	3/14/2002
Piney Creek Habitat Protection	MD	80	0	0	6/20/2001
Total		**44,002**	**27,576**	**100**	
Crowley Island	ME	312	0	0	6/12/2002
Florida Lake Conservation & Recreation Area	ME	152	0	152	6/20/2001
Hooper Pond Conservation Initiative	ME	54	0	0	6/12/2002
Kennebec Estuary	ME	1,572	0	0	9/10/2002
Marsh River - Wade Acquisition	ME	35	0	0	6/12/2002
Middle Bay Habitat Protection: Skolfield Shorelands	ME	77	0	0	6/12/2002
Morong Cove Acquisition	ME	181	0	181	6/20/2001
Presumpscot River Preserve Acquisition	ME	60	0	0	6/12/2002
Total		**2,443**	**0**	**333**	
East Grand Traverse Bay Wetlands Initiative	MI	1,104	0	0	9/21/2001
Lake St. Clair/Western Lake Erie Watershed Project	MI	875	2,223	1,098	9/21/2001
Michigan Upper Peninsula Coastal Wetland II	MI	3,147	86	106	9/21/2001
Round Lake Headwaters Project	MI	486	0	0	6/20/2001
Skaff Parcel Protected Forever	MI	78	0	0	6/20/2001
St. Mary's River Bird Migration Corridor	MI	2,717	0	0	9/10/2002
Susan Creek Project	MI	130	0	0	6/12/2002
Total		**8,537**	**2,309**	**1,204**	

Multistate projects are listed in each state where they occur. Full figures are given with each listing.

U.S. North American Wetlands Conservation Act Projects Arrayed by State
Acres Protected, Restored, and Enhanced in Fiscal Years 2002-2003
[Section 10(1)(A)]

Project Title	State	Acquired Acres	Restored Acres	Enhanced Acres	Date Approved
Centennial Pothole Venture	MN	4,231	2,202	410	3/14/2002
Central Minnesota Grassland Habitats Project	MN	35	250	0	6/12/2002
Comprehensive Bird Conservation, Red River of the North	MN	1,710	3,070	523	3/14/2002
Heron Lake Watershed Project	MN	60	60	0	6/12/2002
Lake Augusta Habitat Restoration	MN	0	500	0	6/20/2001
Minnesota Forest Wetland Restoration Project	MN	0	120	0	6/12/2002
Minnesota USFWS Land Restorations & Enhancements	MN	0	1,275	1,489	6/20/2001
Moberg Wetland - Centennial WPA	MN	0	584	0	6/20/2001
Southern Tallgrass Prairie Wetlands Initiative	MN, IA	1,467	1,393	0	9/10/2002
Transition Zone Grassland Enhancement Project	MN	20	159	0	6/12/2002
Total		**7,523**	**9,613**	**2,422**	
B. K. Leach Memorial Conservation Area Addition	MO	5,706	2,797	0	9/21/2001
Lewis & Clark Floodplain Heritage Partnership I	MO	11,848	8,957	0	3/14/2002
Total		**17,554**	**11,754**	**0**	
Butler Lake Watershed Reforestation & Weir Stabilization	MS	0	948	0	6/20/2001
Grand Bay National Wildlife Refuge	MS	2,700	0	40	6/12/2002
Lower Mississippi Valley Ecosystem III	MS, AR, LA	2,778	11,278	31,617	9/21/2001
O'Keefe WMA Wetlands Restoration	MS	8,562	1,160	375	6/12/2002
Upper Pascagoula Connector Project	MS	2,554	200	0	6/12/2002
Total		**16,594**	**13,586**	**32,032**	
Blackfoot Watershed I	MT	13,453	651	1,918	9/10/2002
Bull River Watershed Protection Project	MT	716	716	0	6/20/2001
Montana Hi-line Prairie Wetland Project	MT	32,935	1,112	26,547	9/21/2001
Rocky Mountain Front Protection Project I	MT	17,934	9,164	0	3/14/2002
Weaver Slough	MT	75	0	0	6/20/2001
Total		**65,113**	**11,643**	**28,465**	
Lower Cape Fear Ricefield Enhancement Project	NC	0	0	155	6/12/2002
Roanoke River Migratory Bird Initiative I	NC, VA	8,942	780	460	3/19/2003
Sea Gate Woods & Carteret County Conservation Partnership	NC	240	0	0	6/20/2001
Sound Investment I	NC, VA	4,179	1,435	596	3/19/2003
Total		**13,361**	**2,215**	**1,211**	
Chase Lake Area Wetland Project V	ND	29,114	161	5,146	9/21/2001
Missouri Coteau Habitat Conservation Project III	ND	43,329	0	0	3/14/2002
Mouse River Watershed Enhancement Project IV	ND	11,468	34	5,599	3/19/2003
North Dakota Great Plains III	ND	0	313	35	3/14/2002
Northern Coteau Project IV	ND	13,540	70	5,338	3/19/2003
Total		**97,451**	**578**	**16,118**	

Multistate projects are listed in each state where they occur. Full figures are given with each listing.

U.S. North American Wetlands Conservation Act Projects Arrayed by State
Acres Protected, Restored, and Enhanced in Fiscal Years 2002-2003
[Section 10(1)(A)]

Project Title	State	Acquired Acres	Restored Acres	Enhanced Acres	Date Approved
Clive Ostenberg Flyway Project	NE, WY	200	0	0	6/20/2001
Middle Missouri River I	NE, IA	4,084	30	456	3/19/2003
Rainwater Basin (East) Partnership Project	NE	1,838	2,205	2,264	9/21/2001
Wood River Roost Wetland	NE	647	332	0	3/14/2002
Total		**6,769**	**2,567**	**2,720**	
Connecticut Lakes Headwaters Project	NH	17,1400	0	0	9/10/2002
Connecticut River: Northern Valley Conservation	NH, VT	82,829	0	0	3/14/2002
Total		**254,229**	**0**	**0**	
Hancock Farm Wetlands Restoration	NJ	0	30	0	6/12/2002
Keep Conservation's Wetland Acquisition	NJ	71	71	0	6/20/2001
Total		**71**	**101**	**0**	
Middle Rio Grande Wetlands Project	NM	58	2,637	0	9/21/2001
Total		**58**	**2,637**	**0**	
Steptoe Valley Wetlands	NV	6,426	2,423	3,553	9/21/2001
Total		**6,426**	**2,423**	**3,553**	
Catatonk Creek Watershed	NY	0	18	0	6/20/2001
Harbor Herons Habitat Restoration in the Saw Mill Wetlands Complex	NY	0	91	0	6/12/2002
North Tonawanda Audubon Nature Preserve (Klydel Wetland)	NY	46	0	0	6/20/2001
Saving the Heart of New York's Great Swamp	NY	1,110	0	0	9/10/2002
Tug Hill Headwaters Conservation Project	NY	44,548	0	0	9/10/2002
Total		**45,704**	**109**	**0**	
Estel Wenrick Wetland Expansion & Connectivity	OH	260	260	0	6/20/2001
Northwest Ohio Wetlands Initiative	OH	1,528	1,596	100	3/14/2002
Total		**1,788**	**1,856**	**100**	
Columbia River Estuary Project	OR, WA	5,268	1,106	612	3/14/2002
Ladd Marsh Wetlands Project	OR	2,159	619	1,139	9/10/2002
Marx Wetland Restoration in the Willamette Valley	OR	66	66	0	6/20/2001
Middle Willamette Valley Floodplain Protection	OR	747	1,320	135	9/21/2001
West Eugene - Long Tom Target Area	OR	771	253	0	3/14/2002
Youngs River Watershed - Walluski River Tidal Swamp	OR	32	32	0	6/12/2002
Total		**9,043**	**3,396**	**1886**	
Chesapeake Bay Initiative II	PA, DE, MD,	0	9,811	0	6/12/2002
Chesapeake Bay Initiative III	PA, DE, MD, VA, WV	0	17,400	0	9/10/2002
Cussewago Bottoms Important Bird Area	PA	100	0	0	6/12/2002
Total		**100**	**27,211**	**0**	

Multistate projects are listed in each state where they occur. Full figures are given with each listing.

U.S. North American Wetlands Conservation Act Projects Arrayed by State
Acres Protected, Restored, and Enhanced in Fiscal Years 2002-2003
[Section 10(1)(A)]

Project Title	State	Acquired Acres	Restored Acres	Enhanced Acres	Date Approved
East Bay Habitat Protection Project II	RI	491	0	16	9/21/2001
Total		**491**	**0**	**16**	
Back Field Rice Field Enhancement Project	SC	0	0	82	6/20/2001
Hickory Top Greentree Reservoir Project	SC	0	0	480	6/12/2002
Restoration of Coastal Plain Depressions, Pinckney Island NWR	SC	0	75	0	6/12/2002
Weetee Bottomlands Acquisition/Restoration	SC	12,449	0	0	9/10/2002
White House Plantation Ricefields Enhancement	SC	0	0	125	6/12/2002
Total		**12,449**	**75**	**687**	
High Plains Wetland Project	SD	0	1,932	0	9/21/2001
Threatened Habitats Project	SD	43,100	3,716	14,000	9/21/2001
Total		**43,100**	**5,648**	**14,000**	
Lower Obion River I	TN	2,936	3,625	0	3/14/2002
Mid-Mississippi Alluvial Valley Bird Conservation Area I	TN	10,713	1,756	1,564	9/21/2001
Mid-Mississippi Alluvial Valley Bird Conservation Area II	TN	2,948	205	1,010	9/10/2002
Mississippi River Habitat Protection Project	TN	1,138	0	0	6/12/2002
Upper Tennessee River I	TN	2,536	326	0	9/10/2002
West Tennessee Migratory Bird Conservation Area	TN	1,139	499	0	6/20/2001
Total		**21,410**	**6,411**	**2,574**	
Laguna Madre	TX	3,080	6,205	18	9/10/2002
Magic Ridge Migratory Bird & Wetlands Sanctuary	TX	624	0	624	6/12/2002
Playa Lakes WMA: Sediment Removal at Cattail Lake & Moist Soil Management	TX	0	18	10	6/12/2002
Port Bolivar Wetlands Protection	TX	1,365	500	310	3/14/2002
Wetlands Restoration Within the West Gulf Coastal Plain	TX	0	3,520	0	9/21/2001
Total		**5,069**	**10,243**	**962**	
Control of Phragmites at Ambassador Duck Club	UT	0	300	0	6/20/2001
Utah Lake Wetlands	UT	387	4,003	0	9/10/2002
Total		**387**	**4,303**	**0**	
Cedar Island Conservation Initiative	VA	48	0	0	6/20/2001
Chesapeake Bay Initiative II	VA, DE, MD, PA, WV	0	9,811	0	6/12/2002
Chesapeake Bay Initiative III	VA, DE, MD, PA, WV	0	17,400	0	9/10/2002
Lackey Farm Restoration & Conservation Project	VA	74	36	0	6/12/2002
Roanoke River Migratory Bird Initiative I	VA, NC	8,942	780	460	3/19/2003
Sound Investment I	VA, NC	4,179	1,435	596	3/19/2003
Southeast Virginia Watersheds Project II	VA	1,156	108	0	9/21/2001
Whitehurst Marsh Acquisition II	VA	715	680	1,315	3/14/2002
Total		**15,114**	**30,250**	**2,371**	

Multistate projects are listed in each state where they occur. Full figures are given with each listing.

U.S. North American Wetlands Conservation Act Projects Arrayed by State
Acres Protected, Restored, and Enhanced in Fiscal Years 2002-2003
[Section 10(1)(A)]

Project Title	State	Acquired Acres	Restored Acres	Enhanced Acres	Date Approved
Connecticut River: Northern Valley Conservation	VT, NH	82,829	0	0	3/14/2002
Total		**82,829**	**0**	**0**	
Acquisition & Restoration of Misner Woods	WA	60	135	0	6/12/2002
Bell Creek Wetland Prairie Restoration Project	WA	0	56	0	6/12/2002
Channeled Scablands Focus Area I	WA	11,152	1,830	10,525	9/21/2001
Christensen Pond Bird Sanctuary	WA	30	0	0	6/20/2001
Columbia River Estuary Project	WA, OR	5,268	1,106	612	3/14/2002
Crow Marsh Project	WA	135	0	0	6/20/2001
Green Cove Basin Wetlands Protection Project	WA	107	0	0	6/20/2001
Hines Marsh Restoration II	WA	127	30	900	6/20/2001
Skagit/Samish Priority Wetlands Habitat Protection & Restoration II	WA	1,010	1,025	0	3/14/2002
Snohomish Wetlands I	WA	2,215	2,150	0	3/19/2003
South Shore Grays Harbor Project	WA	1,001	241	0	9/21/2001
The Port Susan Bay All Bird Initiative	WA	4,122	160	500	9/21/2001
West Hylebos Salmon Acquisition Project	WA	33	0	0	6/20/2001
Willapa Bay II	WA	743	634	0	9/10/2002
Total		**26,003**	**7,367**	**12,537**	
Glacial Habitat Restoration Area IV	WI	2,260	235	999	3/14/2002
Leland Marsh/Baraboo Range Conservation Easement Project	WI	83	0	0	6/12/2002
Lower Chippewa River Wetland Protection Partnership	WI	2,309	150	0	9/10/2002
Scuppernong River Wetland Restoration	WI	20	200	0	6/12/2002
South-central Wisconsin Prairie Pothole Initiative II	WI	1,537	817	975	3/19/2003
Southeast Wisconsin Coastal Habitat Initiative III	WI	1,025	586	1,051	9/21/2001
Superior Coastal Wetland Initiative II	WI	3,095	249	2,574	9/10/2002
Wisconsin Waterfowl Association Shallow Wetland	WI	0	180	0	6/20/2001
Total		**10,329**	**2,417**	**5,599**	
Chesapeake Bay Initiative II	WV, DE, MD, PA, VA	0	9,811	0	6/12/2002
Chesapeake Bay Initiative III	WV, DE, MD, PA, VA	0	17,400	0	9/10/2002
Total		**0**	**27,211**	**0**	
Clive Ostenberg Flyway Project	WY, NE	200	0	0	6/20/2001
Lower Green River Wetland Restoration Project	WY	0	185	0	6/20/2001
Teton River Basin Wetlands Conservation III	WY, ID	1,827	2,663	0	9/10/2002
Total		**2,027**	**2,848**	**0**	

Multistate projects are listed in each state where they occur. Full figures are given with each listing.

Canadian North American Wetlands Conservation Act Projects Arrayed by Province
Acres Protected, Restored, and Enhanced in Fiscal Years 2002-2003
[Section 10(1)(A)]

Project Title	Province	Acquired Acres	Restored Acres	Enhanced Acres	Date Approved
Alberta Critical Wetland & Upland Habitat	AB	9,500	0	1,800	6/12/2002
Alberta Critical Wetland & Upland Habitat	AB	8,000	0	1,000	6/25/2003
Alberta Habitat Program	AB	37,031	0	24,317	6/25/2003
Alberta Habitat Program	AB, BC	28,987	0	36,154	9/21/2001
Alberta Habitat Program	AB, BC	33,800	0	42,156	6/12/2002
Alberta Habitat Program	AB, BC	16,992	0	13,244	9/10/2002
Western Boreal Forest Program	AB, BC, MB, NT, NU, SK, YT	7,000,000	0	50,000	6/12/2002
Western Boreal Forest Program	AB, BC, MB, NT, SK, YT	863,000	0	0	6/25/2003
Total		**7,997,310**	**0**	**168,671**	
Alberta Habitat Program	BC, AB	28,987	0	36,154	9/21/2001
Alberta Habitat Program	BC, AB	33,800	0	42,156	6/12/2002
Alberta Habitat Program	BC, AB	16,992	0	13,244	9/10/2002
Coastal & Intermountain British Columbia	BC	950	0	250	6/12/2002
Conservation of Critical Wetlands & Associated Upland Habitats, Coastal	BC	310	0	600	6/25/2003
Conservation of Wetlands & Associated Upland Habitats, Coastal & Intermountain	BC	515	0	300	9/21/2001
Conservation of Wetlands & Associated Upland Habitats, Coastal	BC	245	0	500	9/10/2002
Critical British Columbia Coastal & Intermountain Wetland Habitats	BC	572	0	116	6/25/2003
Critical British Columbia Coastal & Intermountain Wetland Habitats	BC	3,375	0	242	6/12/2002
Critical Wetlands & Associated Upland Habitats, Intermountain	BC	2,800	0	1,853	6/25/2003
South Okanagan Key Program Areas	BC	150	0	150	9/21/2001
Western Boreal Forest Program	BC, AB, MB, NT, NU, SK, YT	7,000,000	0	50,000	6/12/2002
Western Boreal Forest Program	BC, AB, MB, NT, SK, YT	863,000	0	0	6/25/2003
Total		**7,951,696**	**0**	**145,565**	
Manitoba Critical Upland & Wetland Habitat	MB	8,960	0	1,280	6/12/2002
Manitoba Prairie Parkland Program	MB	9,111	0	6,501	9/21/2001
Manitoba Prairie Parkland Program	MB	9,337	0	6,662	6/12/2002
Manitoba Prairie Parkland Program	MB	18,033	0	12,359	9/10/2002
Manitoba Prairie Parkland Program	MB	32,367	0	21,482	6/25/2003
Potholes Plus Project	MB	6,350	0	25	6/12/2002
Potholes Plus Project	MB	7,900	0	0	6/25/2003
Western Boreal Forest Program	MB, AB, BC, NT, NU, SK, YT	7,000,000	0	50,000	6/12/2002
Western Boreal Forest Program	MB, AB, BC, NT, SK, YT	863,000	0	0	6/25/2003
Total		**7,955,058**	**0**	**98,309**	

Multistate projects are listed in each state where they occur. Full figures are given with each listing.

Canadian North American Wetlands Conservation Act Projects Arrayed by Province
Acres Protected, Restored, and Enhanced in Fiscal Years 2002-2003
[Section 10(1)(A)]

Project Title	Province	Acquired Acres	Restored Acres	Enhanced Acres	Date Approved
Bay of Fundy Habitat Securement Project	NB, NS	600	0	0	6/12/2002
New Brunswick Wetlands	NB	1,496	0	704	9/21/2001
New Brunswick Wetlands Conservation	NB	1,127	0	716	6/12/2002
New Brunswick Wetlands Conservation	NB	720	0	385	9/10/2002
New Brunswick Wetlands Conservation	NB	1,772	0	932	6/25/2003
Northumberland Strait Coastal Wetland Securement	NB, NS, PEI	700	0	0	6/25/2003
Total		**6,415**	**0**	**2,737**	
Newfoundland & Labrador Coastal & Inland Freshwater Wetlands	NF	790	0	79	9/21/2001
Newfoundland & Labrador Coastal & Inland Freshwater Wetlands	NF	610	0	130	6/12/2002
Newfoundland & Labrador Coastal & Inland Freshwater Wetlands	NF	570	0	135	9/10/2002
Newfoundland & Labrador Coastal & Inland Freshwater Wetlands	NF	1,100	0	250	6/25/2003
Total		**3,070**	**0**	**594**	
Bay of Fundy Habitat Securement Project	NS, NB	600	0	0	6/12/2002
Northumberland Strait Coastal Wetland Securement	NS, NB, PEI	700	0	0	6/25/2003
Nova Scotia Coastal & Inland Wetlands	NS	1,221	0	605	9/21/2001
Nova Scotia Coastal & Inland Wetlands	NS	722	0	682	6/12/2002
Nova Scotia Coastal & Inland Wetlands	NS	176	0	104	9/10/2002
Nova Scotia Coastal & Inland Wetlands	NS	635	0	385	6/25/2003
Total		**4,054**	**0**	**1,776**	
Western Boreal Forest Program	NT, AB, BC, MB, NU, SK, YT	7,000,000	0	50,000	6/12/2002
Western Boreal Forest Program	NT, AB, BC, MB, SK, YT	863,000	0	0	6/25/2003
Total		**7,863,000**	**0**	**50,000**	
Western Boreal Forest Program	NU, AB, BC, MB, NT, SK, YT	7,000,000	0	50,000	6/12/2002
Total		**7,000,000**	**0**	**50,000**	
Great Lakes Wetland Habitat Project	ON	375	0	100	6/25/2003
Ontario Regional Project	ON	1,215	0	1,205	9/21/2001
Ontario Regional Project	ON	1,490	0	1,400	6/12/2002
Ontario Regional Project	ON	642	0	600	9/10/2002
Ontario Regional Project	ON	5,420	0	22,04	6/25/2003
Ontario Wetland Habitat Conservation Project	ON	1,000	0	0	6/12/2002
Ontario Wetland Habitat Fund Program	ON	4,000	0	6,000	9/21/2001
Ontario Wetland Habitat Fund Program	ON	4,750	0	5,750	9/10/2002
Total		**18,892**	**0**	**17,259**	

Multistate projects are listed in each state where they occur. Full figures are given with each listing.

Canadian North American Wetlands Conservation Act Projects Arrayed by Province
Acres Protected, Restored, and Enhanced in Fiscal Years 2002-2003
[Section 10(1)(A)]

Project Title	Province	Acquired Acres	Restored Acres	Enhanced Acres	Date Approved
Northumberland Strait Coastal Wetland Securement	PEI, NB, NS	700	0	0	6/25/2003
Prince Edward Island Wetlands in the Agricultural Landscape	PEI	1,371	0	1,029	9/21/2001
Prince Edward Island Wetlands in the Agricultural Landscape	PEI	1,028	0	978	6/12/2002
Prince Edward Island Wetlands in the Agricultural Landscape	PEI	887	0	842	9/10/2002
Prince Edward Island Wetlands in the Agricultural Landscape	PEI	968	0	983	6/25/2003
Total		**4,954**	**0**	**3,832**	
Quebec/St. Lawrence & Adjoining Landscapes	QC	5,700	0	1,300	9/21/2001
Quebec/St. Lawrence & Adjoining Landscapes	QC	1,500	0	1,000	6/12/2002
Quebec/St. Lawrence & Adjoining Landscapes	QC	1,200	0	400	9/10/2002
Quebec/St. Lawrence & Adjoining Landscapes	QC	4,400	0	495	6/25/2003
Quebec Critical Wetland & Upland Habitat	QC	1,000	0	430	6/25/2003
Total		**13,800**	**0**	**3,625**	
Saskatchewan Critical Wetland & Upland Habitat	SK	12,800	0	1,600	6/12/2002
Saskatchewan Habitat Program	SK	36,142	0	30,796	9/21/2001
Saskatchewan Habitat Program	SK	38,650	0	32,939	6/12/2002
Saskatchewan Habitat Program	SK	24,509	0	27,891	9/10/2002
Saskatchewan Habitat Program	SK	58,821	0	59,937	6/25/2003
Saskatchewan Prairie Shores Project	SK	17,500	300	0	9/21/2001
Saskatchewan Prairie Shores Project	SK	20,600	0	500	9/10/2002
Western Boreal Forest Program	SK, AB, BC, MB, NT, NU, YT	7,000,000	0	50,000	6/12/2002
Western Boreal Forest Program	SK, AB, BC, MB, NT, YT	863,000	0	0	6/25/2003
Total		**8,072,022**	**300**	**203,663**	
Western Boreal Forest Program	YT, AB, BC, MB, NT, NU, SK	7,000,000	0	50,000	6/12/2002
Western Boreal Forest Program	YT, AB, BC, MB, NT, SK	863,000	0	0	6/25/2003
Total		**7,863,000**	**0**	**50,000**	

Multistate projects are listed in each state where they occur. Full figures are given with each listing.

Mexican North American Wetlands Conservation Act Projects Arrayed by State
Acres Protected, Restored, and Enhanced in Fiscal Years 2002-2003
[Section 10(1)(A)]

Project Title	State	Acquired Acres	Restored Acres	Enhanced Acres	Date Approved
A Community Partnership - Rio Hardy in the Colorado River Delta	BCN	0	20	0	6/12/2002
Total		**0**	**20**	**0**	
Durangueno Wetlands	DGO	0	0	1,272	6/12/2002
Total		**0**	**0**	**1,272**	
Rio Laja Wetlands Protection Project II	GTO	0	13,000	0	9/10/2002
Rivers Restoration of Five Microwatersheds of La Purisima Watershed	GTO	0	25,722	0	9/10/2002
Total		**0**	**38,722**	**0**	
Establishment of Management, Monitoring, Visitor Center, & Acquisition of Pez Maya	QROO	64	0	0	9/21/2001
Total		**64**	**0**	**0**	
Restoration of Cienega de San Bernardino Watershed, Phase II	SON	1,173	1,173	0	3/14/2002
Total		**1,173**	**1,173**	**0**	
Rancho El Hermalbo	TAMPS	0	0	140	3/14/2002
Rehabilitation of the Anda la Piedra Lagoon, Laguna Madre	TAMPS	0	7,410	0	9/10/2002
Total		**0**	**7,410**	**140**	
La Microcuenca Costera de Chabihau	YUC	0	3,507	0	9/10/2002
Purchase of Land Rights, Birds & Wildlife Habitat	YUC	4,940	0	0	9/21/2001
Restoration, Dzilam State Reserve, Ria Lagartos Biosphere Reserve III	YUC	0	0	7,353	9/10/2002
Restauracion de Cobertura Vegetal, El Palmar, II	YUC	0	12,500	0	9/21/2001
San Crisanto, A Sustainable Development II	YUC	0	98	0	3/14/2002
Total		**4,940**	**16,105**	**7,353**	

13

Migratory Bird Trends
[Section 10(1)(B)]

Each year the United States Fish and Wildlife Service (Service), in conjunction with states, the Canadian Wildlife Service, provincial governments, and other partners, conducts breeding grounds surveys to estimate the size of duck breeding populations. Specialized surveys track trends in the populations of other harvested migratory species such as the mourning dove and the American woodcock. The North American Breeding Bird Survey, conducted annually on approximately 2,900 routes in the United States and Canada by thousands of volunteers, is used to follow changes in the distribution and abundance of many other migratory bird species utilizing wetlands and associated habitats.

Most waterfowl populations remain healthy during the 2002-2003 reporting period of the Act. Wetland conditions in the United States portion of the important duck breeding area known as the Prairie Pothole Region were variable as drier conditions returned to some parts of the United States' north-central plains. Wetland conditions in the Canadian prairies were also variable; however, drought-stricken Alberta and western Saskatchewan experienced relief and dramatically improved wetland conditions following heavy snowfall and spring rains prior to the 2003 breeding season. Effective harvest regulation and millions of acres of habitat conserved through programs such as the North American Waterfowl Management Plan (Plan), the North American Wetlands Conservation Act (Act), the Conservation Reserve Program, and the Wetlands Reserve Program, in conjunction with good precipitation on the prairies, have translated into abundant populations of most prairie breeding ducks over recent years.

The total number of ducks surveyed in 2003 was 36.2 million, only slightly lower than the 36.4 million goal established by the Plan. Six of the 10 most common duck species were at, or exceeded, species-specific Plan goals. Mallard, American wigeon, northern pintail, and scaup populations are below Plan objective levels. Northern pintail and scaup populations remain depressed and concern lingers about the status and future of these species. The scaup population estimate was 41 percent below the Plan's goal and was only slightly improved from the record low estimate of 1998. Pintail, likewise, were 54 percent below the Plan population goal in 2003. Unlike other upland nesting ducks, the pintail population remained depressed and did not respond to improved breeding habitat conditions that occurred during the late 1990s.

Most goose populations continue to thrive; however, three populations of the Canada goose (Atlantic, Southern James Bay, and dusky) continue to be of special concern because of low population abundance or poor reproduction. Since 1995, when hunting seasons were closed on Atlantic Canada geese, northern Quebec breeding pair estimates have increased an average of 28 percent per year. Nesting conditions in the spring of 2002 were poor, however. Many pairs observed during the annual breeding population survey were not nesting. Poor production likely contributed to a lack of growth in population size as recorded by the 2003 survey. In general, however, increase in the size of the Atlantic Population of Canada geese in response to closed and restrictive hunting seasons is encouraging. There is continued concern about problems associated with overabundance of some goose populations including several populations of snow geese and giant (i.e., resident) Canada geese. Harvest

14

management measures have been implemented to address overabundance concerns and are showing some success. Growth in Greater, Western Central Flyway, and Mid-continent Populations of lesser snow geese appears to have been halted by recent regulatory liberalizations. Additional years of monitoring data will be necessary to determine if growth of these populations can be held in check through the regulatory options pursued thus far.

Between 2002-2003, call-count indices of mourning dove populations were relatively stable in the Western and Central Management Units, although call indices declined in the Eastern Unit. Call indices in all three management units indicate no trend over the past 10 years. Call indices in each management unit have declined significantly over the 38-year period of the Mourning Dove Call-Count Survey. Breeding population indices derived through the American Woodcock Singing-ground Survey in 2003 were unchanged from 2002 for both the Eastern and Central Management Regions. Short-term (1993-2003) and long-term (1968-2003) trends in the number of displaying woodcock in both regions indicate significant declines. If current trends in land-use practices persist, continued long-term population declines are likely.

Trends of other migratory bird species vary widely. Of all species groups, grassland nesting birds have exhibited the most consistent negative population trends since the late 1960s, with 61 percent of these species showing significant population declines. These patterns can be explained by extensive loss or degradation of grassland habitat from agricultural uses, as well as increases in haying. Restoration of native grasses or planting of dense-nesting cover under the Plan and funded through the Act has produced positive effects on the density of nesting birds and nest success in the Prairie Pothole Region. These and other critical programs, such as the Conservation Reserve Program and Partners in Flight, provide hope for these beleaguered populations.

As a whole, 64 percent of wetland-dependent migratory bird species show significant increasing long-term population trends. Fourteen percent of these species exhibit significant declining long-term trends. However, data from the North American Breeding Bird Survey are poor for many of these species, and conclusions must be viewed with caution.

Species breeding in mature forested habitats have exhibited a complex spatial pattern of increasing and decreasing trends across North America. In general, increasing population trends predominate in the north-eastern and mid-Atlantic United States, while no patterns are obvious for the central and western portions of the continent. The pattern in the east may be reflective of enlarging and maturing woodlands in this region. Overall, 29 percent of forest species display significant positive trends since the late 1960s.

Each of the above species groups contains both short-distance and neotropical migrants. Short-distance migrants breed and winter north of the United States-Mexico border, whereas neotropical migrants winter south of it. In certain areas where the number of short-distance migrant species is highest, such as the northeast United States, Great Lakes states, and the Canadian prairie, negative population trends predominate for this group. In all, 36 percent of these species exhibit significant decreasing trends. Regional population trends of neotropical migrants are complex and patterns are difficult to discern. Thirty-one percent of neotropical migrant species have exhibited significant negative population trends since the late 1960s.

For many species, the extent to which population trend is driven by the destruction and degradation of wintering habitats south of the United States is unknown. However, it is believed that habitat loss south of the United States border is contributing to the decline of some of these species.

International cooperation is needed to assure the conservation of habitats used by migratory birds throughout their annual cycles. It is through continental programs such as the Plan and Act's grants program that international cooperation can be fostered.

International Agreements
[Section 10(1)(C)]

No progress has been made to establish agreements with officials of other nations in the western hemisphere for the protection of migratory birds.

U.S. North American Wetlands Conservation Act Projects Arrayed by State
Conservation Mechanisms in Fiscal Years 2002-2003
[Section 10(1)(D)]

Project Title	State	Project Type	Conservation Mechanisms	Acres	Years Duration	Date Approved
Agulowak River Protection Project	AK	A, O	fee title	80	permanent	6/20/2001
Izembek NWR Complex I	AK	A	fee title	21,565	permanent	9/21/2001
Izembek NWR Complex II	AK	A	fee title	21,781	permanent	3/19/2003
Spuhn Island Protection Project	AK	A, O	fee title	157	permanent	6/12/2002
Mobile - Tensaw Delta III	AL	A, R, O	fee title	12,682	permanent	3/14/2002
Arkansas Ecoregional Portfolio Sites I	AR	A, E, R, O	fee title	5,211	permanent	9/10/2002
			easement	2,060	permanent	
Choctaw Island	AR	A, R	fee title	8,300	permanent	9/21/2001
Lower Mississippi Valley Ecosystem III	AR, LA, MS	A, E, R, O	easement	2,778	permanent	9/21/2001
Southwest Wildlife Riparian Habitat Protection	AZ	A, E, R, O	fee title	60	permanent	6/20/2001
Bahia Acquisition	CA	A	fee title	639	permanent	9/10/2002
Jacoby Creek Easement Acquisition	CA	A, R	easement	6	permanent	6/20/2001
Lakeview Farms Wetlands Conservation Project	CA	A, R, O	easement	138	permanent	6/12/2002
Poso Creek Flood Plain Wetland Habitat Project	CA	A, E, R	easement	3,510	permanent	3/14/2002
Simmons Slough Wildlife Corridor Acquisition Parcel #1	CA	A	fee title	70	permanent	6/20/2001
Yolo Basin Wetland Habitat Project I	CA	A, E, R, O	fee title	3,753	permanent	3/19/2003
			easement	3,941	permanent	
San Luis Valley Wetland Restoration Project II	CO	A, E, R, O	easement	5,206	permanent	3/19/2003
South Park Valley Premier Wetlands & Mountain Plover Habitat	CO	A, R	fee title	3,470	permanent	3/14/2002
			easement	7,490	permanent	
North Delaware Wetlands Rehab Program - Old Wilmington Marsh	DE	A, E, R	fee title	122	permanent	9/21/2001
			easement	80	permanent	
Burnett Lake Phase - San Felasco Conservation Corridor	FL	A, R	fee title	30	permanent	6/12/2002
Broxton Rocks Expansion Acquisition Project	GA	A	fee title	785	permanent	6/20/2001
Chickasawhatchee Swamp Habitat Conservation	GA	A	fee title	19,700	permanent	3/14/2002
Hawaii Wetlands - Oahu	HI	A, E, R	fee title	4,816	permanent	9/10/2002
Iowa Glaciated Wetlands Initiative	IA	A, R	fee title	2,725	permanent	9/21/2001
			easement	58	permanent	
Middle Missouri River I	IA, NE	A, E, R, O	fee title	3,348	permanent	3/19/2003
			easement	736	permanent	
Southern Tallgrass Prairie Wetlands Initiative	IA, MN	A, R, O	fee title	1,362	permanent	9/10/2002
			easement	105	permanent	
Henry's Fork Wetlands	ID	A, R, O	fee title	161	permanent	3/19/2003
			easement	708	permanent	
Teton River Basin Wetlands Conservation III	ID, WY	A, R, O	easement	1,827	permanent	9/10/2002

Multistate projects are listed in each state where they occur. Full figures are given with each listing.

U.S. North American Wetlands Conservation Act Projects Arrayed by State
Conservation Mechanisms in Fiscal Years 2002-2003
[Section 10(1)(D)]

Project Title	State	Project Type	Conservation Mechanisms	Acres	Years Duration	Date Approved
Aboite Wetland Restoration	IN	A	fee title	97	permanent	6/20/2001
McPherson Valley Wetlands IV	KS	A, E, R, O	fee title	1,295	permanent	9/21/2001
Green River State Forest	KY	A, E, R, O	fee title	1,980	permanent	3/14/2002
Acadiana Park Wetland Preservation	LA	A	fee title	130	permanent	6/12/2002
Lower Mississippi Valley Ecosystem III	LA, AR, MS	A, E, R, O	easement	2,778	permanent	9/21/2001
Pointe - Aux - Chenes Hydrologic Restoration	LA	A, E, R, O	lease	1,454	<10	3/19/2003
O'Keefe Acquisition	MA	A	fee title	25	permanent	6/20/2001
The Ganson Trust Lands	MA	A		215	permanent	6/12/2002
Dividing Creek	MD	A, E, R, O	fee title	5,245	permanent	9/10/2002
Heart of the Chesapeake I	MD	A, R, O	fee title	19,318	permanent	9/21/2001
Heart of the Chesapeake II	MD	A, R, O	fee title	19,359	permanent	3/14/2002
Piney Creek Habitat Protection	MD	A	fee title	80	permanent	6/20/2001
Crowley Island	ME	A, O	fee title	312	permanent	6/12/2002
Florida Lake Conservation & Recreation Area	ME	A, E, O	fee title	152	permanent	6/20/2001
Hooper Pond Conservation Initiative	ME	A, O	fee title	54	permanent	6/12/2002
Kennebec Estuary	ME	A, O	fee title	1,213	permanent	9/10/2002
			easement	360	permanent	
Marsh River - Wade Acquisition	ME	A, O	fee title	35	permanent	6/12/2002
Middle Bay Habitat Protection: Skolfield Shorelands	ME	A	fee title	77	permanent	6/12/2002
Morong Cove Acquisition	ME	A, E	fee title	181	permanent	6/20/2001
Presumpscot River Preserve Acquisition	ME	A	fee title	60	permanent	6/12/2002
East Grand Traverse Bay Wetlands Initiative	MI	A	fee title	782	permanent	9/21/2001
			easement	322	permanent	
Lake St. Clair/Western Lake Erie Watershed Project	MI	A, E, R, O	fee title	845	permanent	9/21/2001
			easement	30	permanent	
Michigan Upper Peninsula Coastal Wetland II	MI	A, E, R, O	fee title	1,794	permanent	9/21/2001
			easement	1,354	permanent	
Round Lake Headwaters Project	MI	A	fee title	486	permanent	6/20/2001
Skaff Parcel Protected Forever	MI	A	fee title	78	permanent	6/20/2001
St. Mary's River Bird Migration Corridor	MI	A, O	fee title	1,915	permanent	9/10/2002
			easement	802	permanent	
Susan Creek Project	MI	A	fee title	130	permanent	6/12/2002
Centennial Pothole Venture	MN	A, E, R, O	fee title	2,230	permanent	3/14/2002
			easement	2,001	permanent	
Central Minnesota Grassland Habitats Project	MN	A, R, O	fee title	35	permanent	6/12/2002
Comprehensive Bird Conservation, Red River of the North	MN	A, E, R, O	fee title	1,180	permanent	3/14/2002
			easement	530	permanent	
Heron Lake Watershed Project	MN	A, R, O	fee title	60	permanent	6/12/2002
Southern Tallgrass Prairie Wetlands Initiative	MN, IA	A, R, O	fee title	1,362	permanent	9/10/2002
			easement	105	permanent	
Transition Zone Grassland Enhancement Project	MN	A, R, O	fee title	20	permanent	6/12/2002

Multistate projects are listed in each state where they occur. Full figures are given with each listing.

U.S. North American Wetlands Conservation Act Projects Arrayed by State Conservation Mechanisms in Fiscal Years 2002-2003
[Section 10(1)(D)]

Project Title	State	Project Type	Conservation Mechanisms	Acres	Years Duration	Date Approved
B. K. Leach Memorial Conservation Area Addition	MO	A, R, O	fee title	2,909	permanent	9/21/2001
			easement	2,797	permanent	
Lewis & Clark Floodplain Heritage Partnership I	MO	A, R, O	fee title	2,952	permanent	3/14/2002
			easement	8,896	permanent	
Grand Bay National Wildlife Refuge	MS	A, E, R, O	fee title	2,700	permanent	6/12/2002
Lower Mississippi Valley Ecosystem III	MS, AR, LA	A, E, R, O	easement	2,778	permanent	9/21/2001
O'keefe WMA Wetlands Restoration	MS	A, E, R, O	fee title	5,640	permanent	6/12/2002
			easement	2,922	permanent	
Upper Pascagoula Connector Project	MS	A, R, O	fee title	2,554	permanent	6/12/2002
Blackfoot Watershed I	MT	A, E, R, O	fee title	1,803	permanent	9/10/2002
			easement	11,650	permanent	
Bull River Watershed Protection Project	MT	A, R	fee title	716	permanent	6/20/2001
Montana Hi-Line Prairie Wetland Project	MT	A, E, R, O	fee title	14,400	permanent	9/21/2001
			easement	18,535	permanent	
Rocky Mountain Front Protection Project I	MT	A, R, O	fee title	7,138	permanent	3/14/2002
			easement	10,796	permanent	
Weaver Slough	MT	A	easement	75	permanent	6/20/2001
Roanoke River Migratory Bird Initiative I	NC, VA	A, E, R, O	fee title	8,942	permanent	3/19/2003
Sea Gate Woods & Carteret County Conservation Partnership	NC	A	fee title	240	permanent	6/20/2001
Sound Investment I	NC, VA	A, E, R, O	fee title	4,179	permanent	3/19/2003
Chase Lake Area Wetland Project V	ND	A, E, R, O	fee title	160	permanent	9/21/2001
			easement	22,185	permanent	
			lease	6,769	< 10 - 25	
Missouri Coteau Habitat Conservation Project III	ND	A	easement	43,329	permanent	3/14/2002
Mouse River Watershed Enhancement Project IV	ND	A, E, R	easement	7,118	permanent	3/19/2003
			lease	4,350	< 10 - 25	
Northern Coteau Project IV	ND	A, E, R, O	easement	8,500	permanent	3/19/2003
			lease	5,040	10	
Clive Ostenberg Flyway Project	NE, WY	A	fee title	200	permanent	6/20/2001
Middle Missouri River I	NE, IA	A, E, R, O	fee title	3,348	permanent	3/19/2003
			easement	736	permanent	
Rainwater Basin (East) Partnership Project	NE	A, E, R	fee title	835	permanent	9/21/2001
			easement	1,003	permanent	
Wood River Roost Wetland	NE	A, R, O	fee title	647	permanent	3/14/2002
Connecticut Lakes Headwaters Project	NH	A, O	fee title	25,000	permanent	9/10/2002
			easement	146,400	permanent	
Connecticut River: Northern Valley Conservation	NH, VT	A, O	fee title	36,100	permanent	3/14/2002
			easement	46,729	permanent	
Keep Conservation's Wetland Acquisition	NJ	A, R, O	fee title	71	permanent	6/20/2001
Middle Rio Grande Wetlands Project	NM	A, R, O	fee title	58	permanent	9/21/2001

Multistate projects are listed in each state where they occur. Full figures are given with each listing.

U.S. North American Wetlands Conservation Act Projects Arrayed by State
Conservation Mechanisms in Fiscal Years 2002-2003
[Section 10(1)(D)]

Project Title	State	Project Type	Conservation Mechanisms	Acres	Years Duration	Date Approved
Steptoe Valley Wetlands	NV	A, E, R, O	fee title	6,426	permanent	9/21/2001
North Tonawanda Audubon Nature Preserve (Klydel Wetland)	NY	A, O	fee title	46	permanent	6/20/2001
Saving the Heart of New York's Great Swamp	NY	A	fee title	799	permanent	9/10/2002
			easement	311	permanent	
Tug Hill Headwaters Conservation Project	NY	A	fee title	14,236	permanent	9/10/2002
			easement	30,312	permanent	
Estel Wenrick Wetland Expansion & Connectivity	OH	A, R, O	easement	260	permanent	6/20/2001
Northwest Ohio Wetlands Initiative	OH	A, E, R, O	fee title	1,103	permanent	3/14/2002
			easement	426	permanent	
Columbia River Estuary Project	OR, WA	A, E, R, O	fee title	4,928	permanent	3/14/2002
			easement	340	permanent	
Ladd Marsh Wetlands Project	OR	A, E, R, O	fee title	1,699	permanent	9/10/2002
			easement	460	26 - permanent	
Marx Wetland Restoration in the Willamette Valley	OR	A, R, O	easement	66	permanent	6/20/2001
Middle Willamette Valley Floodplain Protection	OR	A, E, R, O	fee title	697	permanent	9/21/2001
			easement	50	permanent	
West Eugene - Long Tom Target Area	OR	A, R	fee title	771	permanent	3/14/2002
Youngs River Watershed - Walluski River Tidal Swamp	OR	A, R	fee title	32	permanent	6/12/2002
Cussewago Bottoms Important Bird Area	PA	A, O	fee title	100	permanent	6/12/2002
East Bay Habitat Protection Project II	RI	A, E	fee title	445	permanent	9/21/2001
			easement	46	permanent	
Weetee Bottomlands Acquisition/Restoration	SC	A	fee title	12,449	permanent	9/10/2002
Threatened Habitats Project	SD	A, E, R	easement	43,100	permanent	9/21/2001
Lower Obion River I	TN	A, R	fee title	2,936	permanent	3/14/2002
Mid-Mississippi Alluvial Valley Bird Conservation Area I	TN	A, E, R	fee title	10,713	permanent	9/21/2001
Mid-Mississippi Alluvial Valley Bird Conservation Area II	TN	A, E, R	fee title	2,948	permanent	9/10/2002
Mississippi River Habitat Protection Project	TN	A	fee title	1,138	permanent	6/12/2002
Upper Tennessee River I	TN	A, R	fee title	2,536	permanent	9/10/2002
West Tennessee Migratory Bird Conservation Area	TN	A, R, O	fee title	1,139	permanent	6/20/2001
Laguna Madre	TX	A, E, R, O	fee title	3,080	permanent	9/10/2002
Magic Ridge Migratory Bird & Wetlands Sanctuary	TX	A, E	fee title	624	permanent	6/12/2002
Port Bolivar Wetlands Protection	TX	A, E, R, O	fee title	1,365	permanent	3/14/2002
Utah Lake Wetlands	UT	A, R, O	fee title	237	permanent	9/10/2002
			easement	150	permanent	

Multistate projects are listed in each state where they occur. Full figures are given with each listing.

U.S. North American Wetlands Conservation Act Projects Arrayed by State
Conservation Mechanisms in Fiscal Years 2002-2003
[Section 10(1)(D)]

Project Title	State	Project Type	Conservation Mechanisms	Acres	Years Duration	Date Approved
Cedar Island Conservation Initiative	VA	A	fee title	48	permanent	6/20/2001
Lackey Farm Restoration & Conservation Project	VA	A, R, O	easement	74	permanent	6/12/2002
Roanoke River Migratory Bird Initiative I	VA, NC	A, E, R, O	fee title	8,942	permanent	3/19/2003
Sound Investment I	VA, NC	A, E, R, O	fee title	4,179	permanent	3/19/2003
Southeast Virginia Watersheds Project II	VA	A, R	fee title	1,156	permanent	9/21/2001
Whitehurst Marsh Acquisition II	VA	A, E, R, O	fee title	715	permanent	3/14/2002
Connecticut River: Northern Valley Conservation	VT, NH	A, O	fee title	36,100	permanent	3/14/2002
			easement	46,729	permanent	
Acquisition & Restoration of Misner Woods	WA	A, R	fee title	60	permanent	6/12/2002
Channeled Scablands Focus Area I	WA	A, E, R, O	fee title	10,952	permanent	9/21/2001
			easement	200	permanent	
Christensen Pond Bird Sanctuary	WA	A	fee title	30	permanent	6/20/2001
Columbia River Estuary Project	WA, OR	A, E, R, O	fee title	4,928	permanent	3/14/2002
			easement	340	permanent	
Crow Marsh Project	WA	A	fee title	135	permanent	6/20/2001
Green Cove Basin Wetlands Protection Project	WA	A, O	fee title	47	permanent	6/20/2001
			easement	60	permanent	
Hines Marsh Restoration II	WA	A, E, R	fee title	127	permanent	6/20/2001
Skagit/Samish Priority Wetlands Habitat Protection & Restoration II	WA	A, R, O	fee title	263	permanent	3/14/2002
			easement	747	permanent	
Snohomish Wetlands I	WA	A, R, O	fee title	958	permanent	3/19/2003
			easement	1,257	permanent	
South Shore Grays Harbor Project	WA	A, R	fee title	1,001	permanent	9/21/2001
The Port Susan Bay All Bird Initiative	WA	A, E, R	fee title	4,122	permanent	9/21/2001
West Hylebos Salmon Acquisition Project	WA	A	fee title	33	permanent	6/20/2001
Willapa Bay II	WA	A, R	fee title	566	permanent	9/10/2002
			easement	177	permanent	
Glacial Habitat Restoration Area IV	WI	A, E, R, O	fee title	1,523	permanent	3/14/2002
			easement	736	permanent	
Leland Marsh/Baraboo Range Conservation Easement Project	WI	A	easement	83	permanent	6/12/2002
Lower Chippewa River Wetland Protection Partnership	WI	A, R, O	fee title	1,772	permanent	9/10/2002
			easement	537	permanent	
Scuppernong River Wetland Restoration	WI	A, R	fee title	20	permanent	6/12/2002
South-Central Wisconsin Prairie Pothole Initiative II	WI	A, E, R, O	fee title	1,439	permanent	3/19/2003
			easement	98	permanent	
Southeast Wisconsin Coastal Habitat Initiative III	WI	A, E, R, O	fee title	949	permanent	9/21/2001
			easement	76	permanent	
Superior Coastal Wetland Initiative II	WI	A, E, R, O	fee title	2,410	permanent	9/10/2002
			easement	685	permanent	
Clive Ostenberg Flyway Project	WY, NE	A	fee title	200	permanent	6/20/2001
Teton River Basin Wetlands Conservation III	WY, ID	A, R, O	easement	1,827	permanent	9/10/2002

Multistate projects are listed in each state where they occur. Full figures are given with each listing.

Canadian North American Wetlands Conservation Act Projects Arrayed by Province
Conservation Mechanisms in Fiscal Years 2002-2003
[Section 10(1)(D)]

Project Title	Province	Project Type	Conservation Mechanisms	Acres	Years Duration	Date Approved
Alberta Critical Wetland & Upland Habitat	AB	A, E	fee title	2,450	permanent	6/12/2002
			agreements[1]	7,050	permanent	
Alberta Critical Wetland & Upland Habitat	AB	A, E	fee title	1,480	permanent	6/25/2003
			agreements	6,520	permanent	
Alberta Habitat Program	AB	A, E	fee title	5,793	permanent	6/25/2003
			agreements	31,238	10 - permanent	
Alberta Habitat Program	AB, BC	A, E	fee title	1,687	permanent	9/21/2001
			agreements	27,300	10 - permanent	
Alberta Habitat Program	AB, BC	A, E	fee title	1,967	permanent	6/12/2002
			agreements	31,833	10 - permanent	
Alberta Habitat Program	AB, BC	A, E	fee title	2,407	permanent	9/10/2002
			agreements	14,585	10 - permanent	
Western Boreal Forest Program	AB, BC, MB, NT, NU, SK, YT	A, E	agreements	7,000,000	20 - permanent	6/12/2002
Western Boreal Forest Program	AB, BC, MB, NT, SK, YT	A	agreements	863,000	20 - permanent	6/25/2003
Alberta Habitat Program	BC, AB	A, E	fee title	1,687	permanent	9/21/2001
			agreements[1]	27,300	10 - permanent	
Alberta Habitat Program	BC, AB	A, E	fee title	1,967	permanent	6/12/2002
			agreements	31,833	10 - permanent	
Alberta Habitat Program	BC, AB	A, E	fee title	2,407	permanent	9/10/2002
			agreements	14,585	10 - permanent	
Coastal & Intermountain British Columbia	BC	A, E	fee title	180	permanent	6/12/2002
			agreements	770	30 - permanent	
Conservation of Critical Wetlands & Associated Upland Habitats, Coastal	BC	A, E	fee title	160	permanent	6/25/2003
			agreements	150	30 - permanent	
Conservation of Wetlands & Associated Upland Habitats, Coastal & Intermountain	BC	A, E	fee title	115	permanent	9/21/2001
			agreements	400	30 - permanent	
Conservation of Wetlands & Associated Upland Habitats, Coastal	BC	A, E	fee title	95	permanent	9/10/2002
			agreements	150	10 - permanent	
Critical British Columbia Coastal & Intermountain Wetland Habitats	BC	A, E	fee title	500	permanent	6/25/2003
			agreements	72	10 - permanent	
Critical British Columbia Coastal & Intermountain Wetland Habitats	BC	A, E	fee title	300	permanent	6/12/2002
			agreements	3,075	30 - permanent	
Critical Wetlands & Associated Upland Habitats, Intermountain	BC	A, E	fee title	300	permanent	6/25/2003
			agreements	2,500	30 - permanent	
South Okanagan Key Program Areas	BC	A, E	fee title	100	permanent	9/21/2001
			agreements	50	30 - permanent	
Western Boreal Forest Program	BC, AB, MB, NT, NU, SK, YT	A, E	agreements	7,000,000	20 - permanent	6/12/2002
Western Boreal Forest Program	BC, AB, MB, NT, SK, YT	A	agreements	863,000	20 - permanent	6/25/2003

Multistate projects are listed in each state where they occur. Full figures are given with each listing.

[1]Agreements are undifferentiated combinations of leases, easements, and management agreements.

Canadian North American Wetlands Conservation Act Projects Arrayed by Province
Conservation Mechanisms in Fiscal Years 2002-2003
[Section 10(1)(D)]

Project Title	Province	Project Type	Conservation Mechanisms	Acres	Years Duration	Date Approved
Manitoba Critical Upland & Wetland Habitat	MB	A, E, O	fee title	1,920	permanent	6/12/2002
			easement	7,040	permanent	
Manitoba Prairie Parkland Program	MB	A, E	fee title	1,001	permanent	9/21/2001
			agreements[1]	8,110	10 - permanent	
Manitoba Prairie Parkland Program	MB	A, E	fee title	1,027	permanent	6/12/2002
			agreements	8,310	10 - permanent	
Manitoba Prairie Parkland Program	MB	A, E	fee title	516	permanent	9/10/2002
			agreements	17,517	10 - permanent	
Manitoba Prairie Parkland Program	MB	A, E	fee title	1,919	permanent	6/25/2003
			agreements	30,448	10 - permanent	
Potholes Plus Project	MB	A, E	easement	5,555	20 - permanent	6/12/2002
			agreements	795	10 - permanent	
Potholes Plus Project	MB	A, O	easement	7,900	permanent	6/25/2003
Western Boreal Forest Program	MB, AB, BC, NT, NU, SK, YT	A, E	agreements	7,000,000	20 - permanent	6/12/2002
Western Boreal Forest Program	MB, AB, BC, NT, SK, YT	A	agreements	863,000	20 - permanent	6/25/2003
Bay of Fundy Habitat Securement Project	NB, NS	A	fee title	500	permanent	6/12/2002
			agreements[1]	100	3 - permanent	
New Brunswick Wetlands	NB	A, E	fee title	312	permanent	9/21/2001
			agreements	1,184	10 - 30	
New Brunswick Wetlands Conservation	NB	A, E	fee title	278	permanent	6/12/2002
			agreements	849	10 - 30	
New Brunswick Wetlands Conservation	NB	A, E	fee title	140	permanent	9/10/2002
			agreements	580	10 - 30	
New Brunswick Wetlands Conservation	NB	A, E	fee title	355	permanent	6/25/2003
			agreements	1,417	10 - 30	
Northumberland Strait Coastal Wetland Securement	NB, NS, PEI	A	fee title	600	permanent	6/25/2003
			agreements	100	10 - permanent	
Newfoundland & Labrador Coastal & Inland Freshwater Wetlands	NF	A, E	fee title	90	permanent	9/21/2001
			agreements[1]	700	20 - 30	
Newfoundland & Labrador Coastal & Inland Freshwater Wetlands	NF	A, E	fee title	40	permanent	6/12/2002
			agreements	570	20 - 30	
Newfoundland & Labrador Coastal & Inland Freshwater Wetlands	NF	A, E	agreements	570	20 - 30	9/10/2002
Newfoundland & Labrador Coastal & Inland Freshwater Wetlands	NF	A, E	agreements	1,100	20 - 30	6/25/2003

Multistate projects are listed in each state where they occur. Full figures are given with each listing.

[1]Agreements are undifferentiated combinations of leases, easements, and management agreements.

Canadian North American Wetlands Conservation Act Projects Arrayed by Province
Conservation Mechanisms in Fiscal Years 2002-2003
[Section 10(1)(D)]

Project Title	Province	Project Type	Conservation Mechanisms	Acres	Years Duration	Date Approved
Bay of Fundy Habitat Securement Project	NS, NB	A	fee title	500	permanent	6/12/2002
			agreements[1]	100	3 - permanent	
Northumberland Strait Coastal Wetland Securement	NS, NB, PEI	A	fee title	600	permanent	6/25/2003
			agreements	100	10 - permanent	
Nova Scotia Coastal & Inland Wetlands	NS	A, E	fee title	121	permanent	9/21/2001
			agreements	1,100	15 - 30	
Nova Scotia Coastal & Inland Wetlands	NS	A, E	fee title	40	permanent	6/12/2002
			agreements	682	15 - 30	
Nova Scotia Coastal & Inland Wetlands	NS	A, E	fee title	72	permanent	9/10/2002
			agreements	104	15 - 30	
Nova Scotia Coastal & Inland Wetlands	NS	A, E	fee title	250	permanent	6/25/2003
			agreements	385	15 - 30	
Western Boreal Forest Program	NT, AB, BC, MB, NU, SK, YT	A, E	agreements[1]	7,000,000	20 - permanent	6/12/2002
Western Boreal Forest Program	NT, AB, BC, MB, SK, YT	A	agreements	863,000	20 - permanent	6/25/2003
Western Boreal Forest Program	NU, AB, BC, MB, NT, SK, YT	A, E	agreements[1]	7,000,000	20 - permanent	6/12/2002
Great Lakes Wetland Habitat Project	ON	A, E	fee title	275	permanent	6/25/2003
			agreements[1]	100	permanent	
Ontario Regional Project	ON	A, E	fee title	205	permanent	9/21/2001
			agreements	1,010	10	
Ontario Regional Project	ON	A, E	fee title	420	permanent	6/12/2002
			agreements	1,070	10 - permanent	
Ontario Regional Project	ON	A, E	fee title	180	permanent	9/10/2002
			agreements	462	10 - permanent	
Ontario Regional Project	ON	A, E	fee title	810	permanent	6/25/2003
			agreements	4,610	20 - permanent	
Ontario Wetland Habitat Conservation Project	ON	A, O	fee title	750	permanent	6/12/2002
			easement	250	999	
Ontario Wetland Habitat Fund Program	ON	A, E	agreements	4,000	15 - permanent	9/21/2001
Ontario Wetland Habitat Fund Program	ON	A, E	agreements	4,750	10	9/10/2002
Northumberland Strait Coastal Wetland Securement	PEI, NB, NS	A	fee title	600	permanent	6/25/2003
			agreements[1]	100	10 - permanent	
Prince Edward Island Wetlands in the Agricultural Landscape	PEI	A, E	fee title	342	permanent	9/21/2001
			agreements	1,029	15 - permanent	
Prince Edward Island Wetlands in the Agricultural Landscape	PEI	A, E	fee title	50	permanent	6/12/2002
			agreements	978	15 - permanent	
Prince Edward Island Wetlands in the Agricultural Landscape	PEI	A, E	fee title	45	permanent	9/10/2002
			agreements	842	15 - permanent	
Prince Edward Island Wetlands in the Agricultural	PEI	A, E	fee title	112	permanent	6/25/2003
			agreements	856	15 - permanent	

Multistate projects are listed in each state where they occur. Full figures are given with each listing.

[1]Agreements are undifferentiated combinations of leases, easements, and management agreements.

Canadian North American Wetlands Conservation Act Projects Arrayed by Province
Conservation Mechanisms in Fiscal Years 2002-2003
[Section 10(1)(D)]

Project Title	Province	Project Type	Conservation Mechanisms	Acres	Years Duration	Date Approved
Quebec/St. Lawrence & Adjoining Landscapes	QC	A, E	fee title	5,000	permanent	9/21/2001
			agreements[1]	700	5 - 30	
Quebec/St. Lawrence & Adjoining Landscapes	QC	A, E	fee title	800	permanent	6/12/2002
			agreements	700	10 - 30	
Quebec/St. Lawrence & Adjoining Landscapes	QC	A, E	fee title	800	permanent	9/10/2002
			agreements	400	10 - 30	
Quebec/St. Lawrence & Adjoining Landscapes	QC	A, E	fee title	3,600	permanent	6/25/2003
			agreements	800	10 - 30	
Quebec Critical Wetland & Upland Habitat	QC	A, E, O	fee title	1,000	permanent	6/25/2003
Saskatchewan Critical Wetland & Upland Habitat	SK	A, E	fee title	2,300	permanent	6/12/2002
			agreements[1]	10,500	permanent	
Saskatchewan Habitat Program	SK	A, E	fee title	11,493	permanent	9/21/2001
			agreements	24,649	6 - 25	
Saskatchewan Habitat Program	SK	A, E	fee title	12,318	permanent	6/12/2002
			agreements	26,332	6 - 25	
Saskatchewan Habitat Program	SK	A, E	fee title	3,185	permanent	9/10/2002
			agreements	21,324	6 - 25	
Saskatchewan Habitat Program	SK	A, E	fee title	7,998	permanent	6/25/2003
			agreements	50,823	6 - 25	
Saskatchewan Prairie Shores Project	SK	A, R	agreements	17,500	10 - permanent	9/21/2001
Saskatchewan Prairie Shores Project	SK	A, E	fee title	600	permanent	9/10/2002
			agreements	20,000	10 - permanent	
Western Boreal Forest Program	SK, AB, BC, MB, NT, NU, YT	A, E	agreements	7,000,000	20 - permanent	6/12/2002
Western Boreal Forest Program	SK, AB, BC, MB, NT, YT	A	agreements	863,000	20 - permanent	6/25/2003
Western Boreal Forest Program	YT, AB, BC, MB, NT, NU, SK	A, E	agreements[1]	7,000,000	20 - permanent	6/12/2002
Western Boreal Forest Program	YT, AB, BC, MB, NT, SK	A	agreements	863,000	20 - permanent	6/25/2003

Multistate projects are listed in each state where they occur. Full figures are given with each listing.
[1]Agreements are undifferentiated combinations of leases, easements, and management agreements.

Mexican North American Wetlands Conservation Act Projects Arrayed by State Conservation Mechanisms in Fiscal Years 2002-2003
[Section 10(1)(D)]

Project Title	State	Project Type	Conservation Mechanisms	Acres	Years Duration	Date Approved
Establishment of Management, Monitoring, Visitor Center, & Acquisition of Pez Maya	QROO	A	fee title	64	permanent	9/21/2001
Restoration of Cienega De San Bernardino Watershed, Phase II	SON	A, R	fee title	1,173	permanent	3/14/2002
Purchase of Land Rights, Birds & Wildlife Habitat	YUC	A, O	fee title	4,940	permanent	9/21/2001

Financial Statements
[Section 10(2)]

Fiscal Year 2002

Receipts

FY 2001 Interest		$26,651,244[1]
FY 2002 Appropriation		$43,500,000
FY 2001 Appropriation Carryover		$6,981,971
FY 2002 Fines, Penalties, Forfeitures		$517,635
FY 2002 Coastal Funds		$13,040,460
FY 2001 Coastal Funds Carryover		$1,191,433
	Total	**$91,882,743**

Debits

Administration		$3,218,117
Project Obligations:		
	Canada	$212,670
	Mexico	$2,599,011
	United States	$35,173,220
	Total	**$41,203,018**

Fiscal Year 2003

Receipts

FY 2002 Interest		$29,180,473[2]
FY 2003 Appropriation		$38,309,360
FY 2002 Appropriation Carryover		$33,874,380
FY 2003 Fines, Penalties, Forfeitures		$525,959
FY 2003 Coastal Funds		$12,201,020
FY 2002 Coastal Funds Carryover		$3,169,197
	Total	**$117,260,389**

Debits

Administration		$3,411,434
Project Obligations:		
	Canada	$50,712,187
	Mexico	$3,479,812
	United States	$48,952,432
	Total	**$106,555,865**

---

[1] Includes funds unobligated in Fiscal Year 2001 and accrued interest during Fiscal Year 2001, which became available at the start of Fiscal Year 2002.

[2] Includes funds unobligated in Fiscal Year 2002 and accrued interest during Fiscal Year 2002, which became available at the start of Fiscal Year 2003.

U.S. North American Wetlands Conservation Act Projects Arrayed by State
Federal and Partner Dollars Invested in Fiscal Years 2002-2003
[Section 10(2)]

Project Title	State	Project Type	Grant Amount	Partner Amount	Total Amount	Date Approved
Agulowak River Protection Project	AK	A, O	$50,000	$111,500	$161,500	6/20/2001
Izembek NWR Complex I	AK	A	$1,000,000	$2,000,000	$3,000,000	9/21/2001
Izembek NWR Complex II	AK	A	$987,000	$2,000,000	$2,987,000	3/19/2003
Spuhn Island Protection Project	AK	A, O	$50,000	$403,500	$453,500	6/12/2002
Total			**$2,087,000**	**$4,515,000**	**$6,602,000**	
Mobile - Tensaw Delta III	AL	A, R, O	$1,000,000	$5,913,200	$6,913,200	3/14/2002
Total			**$1,000,000**	**$5,913,200**	**$6,913,200**	
Arkansas Ecoregional Portfolio Sites I	AR	A, E, R, O	$957,419	$10,715,100	$11,672,519	9/10/2002
Choctaw Island	AR	A, R	$300,000	$7,380,580	$7,680,580	9/21/2001
Lower Mississippi Valley Ecosystem III	AR, LA, MS	A, E, R, O	$999,667	$3,592,576	$4,592,243	9/21/2001
Total			**$2,257,086**	**$21,688,256**	**$23,945,342**	
Southwest Wildlife Riparian Habitat Protection	AZ	A, E, R, O	$50,000	$477,000	$527,000	6/20/2001
Total			**$50,000**	**$477,000**	**$527,000**	
Bahia Acquisition	CA	A	$1,000,000	$14,400,000	$15,400,000	9/10/2002
Butte Basin & Colusa Trough Wetland Habitat II	CA	E, R, O	$999,236	$2,394,585	$3,393,821	9/10/2002
Jacoby Creek Easement Acquisition	CA	A, R	$32,000	$73,950	$105,950	6/20/2001
Lakeview Farms Wetlands Conservation Project	CA	A, R, O	$50,000	$445,527	$495,527	6/12/2002
Poso Creek Flood Plain Wetland Habitat Project	CA	A, E, R	$1,000,000	$6,566,740	$7,566,740	3/14/2002
Simmons Slough Wildlife Corridor Acquisition Parcel #1	CA	A	$50,000	$1,577,850	$1,627,850	6/20/2001
Yolo & Delta Basins Wetlands Restoration & Enhancement	CA	E, R, O	$969,569	$2,811,794	$3,781,363	3/19/2003
Yolo Basin Wetland Habitat Project I	CA	A, E, R, O	$1,000,000	$10,210,500	$11,210,500	3/19/2003
Total			**$5,100,805**	**$38,480,946**	**$43,581,751**	
San Luis Valley Wetland Restoration Project II	CO	A, E, R, O	$1,000,000	$2,793,210	$3,793,210	3/19/2003
South Park Valley Premier Wetlands & Mountain Plover Habitat	CO	A, R	$1,000,000	$2,766,000	$3,766,000	3/14/2002
Total			**$2,000,000**	**$5,559,210**	**$7,559,210**	
Inland Marsh Restoration In Natchaug State Forest	CT	R	$25,000	$45,000	$70,000	6/12/2002
Total			**$25,000**	**$45,000**	**$70,000**	
Chesapeake Bay Initiative II	DE, MD, PA, VA, WV	R	$533,000	$1,532,628	$2,065,628	6/12/2002
Chesapeake Bay Initiative III	DE, MD, PA, VA, WV	R	$1,000,000	$2,006,410	$3,006,410	9/10/2002
Delaware Coastal Plain Restoration Project	DE	R	$50,000	$60,000	$110,000	6/20/2001
North Delaware Wetlands Rehab Program - Old Wilmington Marsh	DE	A, E, R	$891,000	$1,877,500	$2,768,500	9/21/2001
Total			**$2,474,000**	**$5,476,538**	**$7,950,538**	

Multistate projects are listed in each state where they occur. Full figures are given with each listing.

U.S. North American Wetlands Conservation Act Projects Arrayed by State
Federal and Partner Dollars Invested in Fiscal Years 2002-2003
[Section 10(2)]

Project Title	State	Project Type	Grant Amount	Partner Amount	Total Amount	Date Approved
Burnett Lake Phase - San Felasco Conservation Corridor	FL	A, R	$40,000	$95,000	$135,000	6/12/2002
Hammock Point Marsh Restoration at Tomoka State Park	FL	R	$49,296	$78,125	$127,421	6/20/2001
Historic Cypress Forest/Swamp Restoration	FL	R	$50,000	$205,612	$255,612	6/20/2001
Total			**$139,296**	**$378,737**	**$518,033**	
Broxton Rocks Expansion Acquisition Project	GA	A	$50,000	$101,500	$151,500	6/20/2001
Chickasawhatchee Swamp Habitat Conservation	GA	A	$1,000,000	$22,315,000	$23,315,000	3/14/2002
Youmans Bird Pond Causeway Restoration	GA	R	$47,149	$47,149	$94,298	6/12/2002
Total			**$1,097,149**	**$22,463,649**	**$23,560,798**	
Hamakua Marsh Ecosystem Restoration & Community Development	HI	R	$50,000	$160,000	$210,000	6/20/2001
Hawaii Wetlands - Oahu	HI	A, E, R	$983,666	$14,306,292	$15,289,958	9/10/2002
Na Pohaku O Hauwahine Wetland Restoration In Kawai Nui Marsh	HI	R	$25,000	$109,990	$134,990	6/20/2001
Total			**$1,058,666**	**$14,576,282**	**$15,634,948**	
Iowa Glaciated Wetlands Initiative	IA	A, R	$700,000	$2,131,117	$2,831,117	9/21/2001
Iowa Prairie Pothole Wetland Development Project	IA	E, O	$50,000	$126,891	$176,891	6/12/2002
Middle Missouri River I	IA, NE	A, E, R, O	$999,944	$2,110,887	$3,110,831	3/19/2003
Southern Tallgrass Prairie Wetlands Initiative	IA, MN	A, R, O	$1,000,000	$1,430,192	$2,430,192	9/10/2002
Total			**$2,749,944**	**$5,799,087**	**$8,549,031**	
Henry's Fork Wetlands	ID	A, R, O	$1,000,000	$2,319,076	$3,319,076	3/19/2003
Teton River Basin Wetlands Conservation III	ID, WY	A, R, O	$1,000,000	$5,415,098	$6,415,098	9/10/2002
Total			**$2,000,000**	**$7,734,174**	**$9,734,174**	
Lower Kaskaskia River Wetland Restoration	IL	R, O	$44,000	$135,687	$179,687	6/12/2002
Midewin Dolomitic Wetland & Prairie Restoration	IL	R	$50,000	$135,294	$185,294	6/12/2002
Nygren Riparian Wetland Restoration	IL	R	$50,000	$321,497	$371,497	6/20/2001
Rollins Savanna Wetland Restoration Project	IL	R	$50,000	$513,060	$563,060	6/12/2002
Total			**$194,000**	**$1,105,538**	**$1,299,538**	
Aboite Wetland Restoration	IN	A	$50,000	$86,005	$136,005	6/20/2001
Total			**$50,000**	**$86,005**	**$136,005**	
McPherson Valley Wetlands IV	KS	A, E, R, O	$557,135	$1,428,172	$1,985,307	9/21/2001
Total			**$557,135**	**$1,428,172**	**$1,985,307**	
Green River State Forest	KY	A, E, R, O	$800,000	$1,655,150	$2,455,150	3/14/2002
Total			**$800,000**	**$1,655,150**	**$2,455,150**	

Multistate projects are listed in each state where they occur. Full figures are given with each listing.

U.S. North American Wetlands Conservation Act Projects Arrayed by State
Federal and Partner Dollars Invested in Fiscal Years 2002-2003
[Section 10(2)]

Project Title	State	Project Type	Grant Amount	Partner Amount	Total Amount	Date Approved
Acadiana Park Wetland Preservation	LA	A	$50,000	$78,500	$128,500	6/12/2002
Chenier Plain Coastal Wetlands Restoration	LA	E, R, O	$999,364	$2,156,303	$3,155,667	3/14/2002
Louisiana Coastal Wetlands II	LA	E, R	$1,000,000	$1,497,260	$2,497,260	3/19/2003
Lower Mississippi Valley Ecosystem III	LA, AR, MS	A, E, R, O	$999,667	$3,592,576	$4,592,243	9/21/2001
Pointe - Aux - Chenes Hydrologic Restoration	LA	A, E, R, O	$992,914	$2,186,354	$3,179,268	3/19/2003
Total			**$4,041,945**	**$9,510,993**	**$13,552,938**	
Nulands Neck Acquisition	MA	R	$50,000	$450,000	$500,000	6/12/2002
O'Keefe Acquisition	MA	A	$35,000	$65,000	$100,000	6/20/2001
Salt Marsh Restoration & Enhancement - Plum Island Sound - Great Marsh	MA	R	$45,000	$50,000	$95,000	6/12/2002
The Ganson Trust Lands	MA	A	$50,000	$310,500	$360,500	6/12/2002
Total			**$180,000**	**$875,500**	**$1,055,500**	
Chesapeake Bay Initiative II	MD, DE, PA, VA, WV	R	$533,000	$1,532,628	$2,065,628	6/12/2002
Chesapeake Bay Initiative III	MD, DE, PA, VA, WV	R	$1,000,000	$2,006,410	$3,006,410	9/10/2002
Dividing Creek	MD	A, E, R, O	$1,000,000	$4,078,320	$5,078,320	9/10/2002
Heart of the Chesapeake I	MD	A, R, O	$1,000,000	$10,653,000	$11,653,000	9/21/2001
Heart of the Chesapeake II	MD	A, R, O	$991,000	$10,650,000	$11,641,000	3/14/2002
Piney Creek Habitat Protection	MD	A	$50,000	$165,000	$215,000	6/20/2001
Total			**$4,574,000**	**$29,085,358**	**$33,659,358**	
Crowley Island	ME	A, O	$50,000	$320,000	$370,000	6/12/2002
Florida Lake Conservation & Recreation Area	ME	A, E, O	$50,000	$401,000	$451,000	6/20/2001
Hooper Pond Conservation Initiative	ME	A, O	$12,500	$36,500	$49,000	6/12/2002
Kennebec Estuary	ME	A, O	$1,000,000	$2,830,500	$3,830,500	9/10/2002
Marsh River - Wade Acquisition	ME	A, O	$50,000	$104,800	$154,800	6/12/2002
Middle Bay Habitat Protection: Skolfield Shorelands	ME	A	$50,000	$515,000	$565,000	6/12/2002
Morong Cove Acquisition	ME	A, E	$50,000	$170,000	$220,000	6/20/2001
Presumpscot River Preserve Acquisition	ME	A	$50,000	$1,071,900	$1,121,900	6/12/2002
Total			**$1,312,500**	**$5,449,700**	**$6,762,200**	
East Grand Traverse Bay Wetlands Initiative	MI	A	$1,000,000	$3,050,000	$4,050,000	9/21/2001
Lake St. Clair/Western Lake Erie Watershed Project	MI	A, E, R, O	$1,000,000	$2,511,672	$3,511,672	9/21/2001
Michigan Upper Peninsula Coastal Wetland II	MI	A, E, R, O	$833,817	$3,258,692	$4,092,509	9/21/2001
Round Lake Headwaters Project	MI	A	$50,000	$3,616,000	$3,666,000	6/20/2001
Skaff Parcel Protected Forever	MI	A	$20,000	$144,500	$164,500	6/20/2001
St. Mary's River Bird Migration Corridor	MI	A, O	$850,000	$4,792,400	$5,642,400	9/10/2002
Susan Creek Project	MI	A	$50,000	$550,000	$600,000	6/12/2002
Total			**$3,803,817**	**$17,923,264**	**$21,727,081**	

Multistate projects are listed in each state where they occur. Full figures are given with each listing.

U.S. North American Wetlands Conservation Act Projects Arrayed by State
Federal and Partner Dollars Fiscal Years Invested in 2002-2003
[Section 10(2)]

Project Title	State	Project Type	Grant Amount	Partner Amount	Total Amount	Date Approved
Centennial Pothole Venture	MN	A, E, R, O	$1,000,000	$6,183,715	$7,183,715	3/14/2002
Central Minnesota Grassland Habitats Project	MN	A, R, O	$50,000	$57,218	$107,218	6/12/2002
Comprehensive Bird Conservation, Red River of the North	MN	A, E, R, O	$798,335	$2,240,873	$3,039,208	3/14/2002
Heron Lake Watershed Project	MN	A, R, O	$50,000	$77,000	$127,000	6/12/2002
Lake Augusta Habitat Restoration	MN	R	$37,500	$71,281	$108,781	6/20/2001
Minnesota Forest Wetland Restoration Project	MN	R, O	$50,000	$127,570	$177,570	6/12/2002
Minnesota USFWS Land Restorations & Enhancements	MN	E, R	$50,000	$89,295	$139,295	6/20/2001
Moberg Wetland - Centennial WPA	MN	R, O	$49,750	$240,053	$289,803	6/20/2001
Southern Tallgrass Prairie Wetlands Initiative	MN, IA	A, R, O	$1,000,000	$1,430,192	$2,430,192	9/10/2002
Transition Zone Grassland Enhancement Project	MN	A, R, O	$50,000	$54,957	$104,957	6/12/2002
Total			**$3,135,585**	**$10,572,154**	**$13,707,739**	
B. K. Leach Memorial Conservation Area Addition	MO	A, R, O	$999,998	$5,662,845	$6,662,843	9/21/2001
Lewis & Clark Floodplain Heritage Partnership I	MO	A, R, O	$970,000	$5,820,895	$6,790,895	3/14/2002
Total			**$1,969,998**	**$11,483,740**	**$13,453,738**	
Butler Lake Watershed Reforestation & Weir Stabilization	MS	R	$50,000	$105,700	$155,700	6/20/2001
Grand Bay National Wildlife Refuge	MS	A, E, R, O	$533,000	$3,800,000	$4,333,000	6/12/2002
Lower Mississippi Valley Ecosystem III	MS, AR, LA	A, E, R, O	$999,667	$3,592,576	$4,592,243	9/21/2001
O'Keefe WMA Wetlands Restoration	MS	A, E, R, O	$652,933	$3,174,550	$3,827,483	6/12/2002
Upper Pascagoula Connector Project	MS	A, R, O	$855,842	$2,045,766	$2,901,608	6/12/2002
Total			**$3,091,442**	**$12,718,592**	**$15,810,034**	
Blackfoot Watershed I	MT	A, E, R, O	$1,000,000	$4,929,735	$5,929,735	9/10/2002
Bull River Watershed Protection Project	MT	A, R	$50,000	$150,242	$200,242	6/20/2001
Montana Hi-Line Prairie Wetland Project	MT	A, E, R, O	$1,000,000	$2,747,060	$3,747,060	9/21/2001
Rocky Mountain Front Protection Project I	MT	A, R, O	$1,000,000	$4,645,617	$5,645,617	3/14/2002
Weaver Slough	MT	A	$50,000	$100,000	$150,000	6/20/2001
Total			**$3,100,000**	**$12,572,654**	**$15,672,654**	
Lower Cape Fear Ricefield Enhancement Project	NC	E	$50,000	$70,000	$120,000	6/12/2002
Roanoke River Migratory Bird Initiative I	NC, VA	A, E, R, O	$965,339	$2,706,924	$3,672,263	3/19/2003
Sea Gate Woods & Carteret County Conservation Partnership	NC	A	$50,000	$104,800	$154,800	6/20/2001
Sound Investment I	NC, VA	A, E, R, O	$1,000,000	$2,354,991	$3,354,991	3/19/2003
Total			**$2,065,339**	**$5,236,715**	**$7,302,054**	
Chase Lake Area Wetland Project V	ND	A, E, R, O	$1,000,000	$1,297,380	$2,297,380	9/21/2001
Missouri Coteau Habitat Conservation Project III	ND	A	$800,000	$839,247	$1,639,247	3/14/2002
Mouse River Watershed Enhancement Project IV	ND	A, E, R	$360,000	$615,532	$975,532	3/19/2003
North Dakota Great Plains III	ND	E, R	$200,000	$368,771	$568,771	3/14/2002
Northern Coteau Project IV	ND	A, E, R, O	$618,000	$928,670	$1,546,670	3/19/2003
Total			**$2,978,000**	**$4,049,600**	**$7,027,600**	

Multistate projects are listed in each state where they occur. Full figures are given with each listing.

U.S. North American Wetlands Conservation Act Projects Arrayed by State
Federal and Partner Dollars Invested in Fiscal Years 2002-2003
[Section 10(2)]

Project Title	State	Project Type	Grant Amount	Partner Amount	Total Amount	Date Approved
Clive Ostenberg Flyway Project	NE, WY	A	$50,000	$250,000	$300,000	6/20/2001
Middle Missouri River I	NE, IA	A, E, R, O	$999,944	$2,110,887	$3,110,831	3/19/2003
Rainwater Basin (East) Partnership Project	NE	A, E, R	$724,610	$2,662,937	$3,387,547	9/21/2001
Wood River Roost Wetland	NE	A, R, O	$560,000	$1,456,021	$2,016,021	3/14/2002
Total			**$2,334,554**	**$6,479,845**	**$8,814,399**	
Connecticut Lakes Headwaters Project	NH	A, O	$1,000,000	$6,075,000	$7,075,000	9/10/2002
Connecticut River: Northern Valley Conservation	NH, VT	A, O	$914,000	$12,757,000	$13,671,000	3/14/2002
Total			**$1,914,000**	**$18,832,000**	**$20,746,000**	
Hancock Farm Wetlands Restoration	NJ	R	$24,835	$39,690	$64,525	6/12/2002
Keep Conservation's Wetland Acquisition	NJ	A, R, O	$45,000	$71,061	$116,061	6/20/2001
Total			**$69,835**	**$110,751**	**$180,586**	
Middle Rio Grande Wetlands Project	NM	A, R, O	$1,000,000	$2,201,087	$3,201,087	9/21/2001
Total			**$1,000,000**	**$2,201,087**	**$3,201,087**	
Steptoe Valley Wetlands	NV	A, E, R, O	$500,000	$1,036,372	$1,536,372	9/21/2001
Total			**$500,000**	**$1,036,372**	**$1,536,372**	
Catatonk Creek Watershed	NY	R	$20,000	$20,707	$40,707	6/20/2001
Harbor Herons Habitat Restoration in the Saw Mill Wetlands Complex	NY	R	$50,000	$289,850	$339,850	6/12/2002
North Tonawanda Audubon Nature Preserve (Klydel Wetland)	NY	A, O	$49,981	$242,720	$292,701	6/20/2001
Saving the Heart of New York's Great Swamp	NY	A	$940,000	$2,521,975	$3,461,975	9/10/2002
Tug Hill Headwaters Conservation Project	NY	A	$650,000	$4,825,000	$5,475,000	9/10/2002
Total			**$1,709,981**	**$7,900,252**	**$9,610,233**	
Estel Wenrick Wetland Expansion & Connectivity	OH	A, R, O	$50,000	$128,288	$178,288	6/20/2001
Northwest Ohio Wetlands Initiative	OH	A, E, R, O	$1,000,000	$5,376,348	$6,376,348	3/14/2002
Total			**$1,050,000**	**$5,504,636**	**$6,554,636**	
Columbia River Estuary Project	OR, WA	A, E, R, O	$997,000	$7,653,553	$8,650,553	3/14/2002
Ladd Marsh Wetlands Project	OR	A, E, R, O	$1,000,000	$3,348,165	$4,348,165	9/10/2002
Marx Wetland Restoration in the Willamette Valley	OR	A, R, O	$35,000	$231,509	$266,509	6/20/2001
Middle Willamette Valley Floodplain Protection	OR	A, E, R, O	$901,400	$2,253,575	$3,154,975	9/21/2001
West Eugene - Long Tom Target Area	OR	A, R	$1,000,000	$11,383,819	$12,383,819	3/14/2002
Youngs River Watershed - Walluski River Tidal Swamp	OR	A, R	$50,000	$54,200	$104,200	6/12/2002
Total			**$3,983,400**	**$24,924,821**	**$28,908,221**	
Chesapeake Bay Initiative II	PA, DE, MD, VA, WV	R	$533,000	$1,532,628	$2,065,628	6/12/2002
Chesapeake Bay Initiative III	PA, DE, MD, VA, WV	R	$1,000,000	$2,006,410	$3,006,410	9/10/2002
Cussewago Bottoms Important Bird Area	PA	A, O	$18,572	$70,728	$89,300	6/12/2002
Total			**$1,551,572**	**$3,609,766**	**$5,161,338**	

Multistate projects are listed in each state where they occur. Full figures are given with each listing.

U.S. North American Wetlands Conservation Act Projects Arrayed by State
Federal and Partner Dollars Invested in Fiscal Years 2002-2003
[Section 10(2)]

Project Title	State	Project Type	Grant Amount	Partner Amount	Total Amount	Date Approved
East Bay Habitat Protection Project II	RI	A, E	$1,000,000	$3,340,425	$4,340,425	9/21/2001
Total			**$1,000,000**	**$3,340,425**	**$4,340,425**	
Back Field Rice Field Enhancement Project	SC	E	$50,000	$61,637	$111,637	6/20/2001
Hickory Top Greentree Reservoir Project	SC	E	$50,000	$257,500	$307,500	6/12/2002
Restoration of Coastal Plain Depressions, Pinckney Island NWR	SC	R	$47,900	$130,797	$178,697	6/12/2002
Weetee Bottomlands Acquisition/Restoration	SC	A	$1,000,000	$7,563,575	$8,563,575	9/10/2002
White House Plantation Ricefields Enhancement	SC	E	$39,050	$58,472	$97,522	6/12/2002
Total			**$1,186,950**	**$8,071,981**	**$9,258,931**	
High Plains Wetland Project	SD	R	$890,000	$2,123,679	$3,013,679	9/21/2001
Threatened Habitats Project	SD	A, E, R	$905,000	$6,390,000	$7,295,000	9/21/2001
Total			**$1,795,000**	**$8,513,679**	**$10,308,679**	
Lower Obion River I	TN	A, R	$1,000,000	$4,686,994	$5,686,994	3/14/2002
Mid-Mississippi Alluvial Valley Bird Conservation Area I	TN	A, E, R	$1,000,000	$5,319,651	$6,319,651	9/21/2001
Mid-Mississippi Alluvial Valley Bird Conservation Area II	TN	A, E, R	$1,000,000	$3,035,740	$4,035,740	9/10/2002
Mississippi River Habitat Protection Project	TN	A	$50,000	$166,000	$216,000	6/12/2002
Upper Tennessee River I	TN	A, R	$1,000,000	$3,479,088	$4,479,088	9/10/2002
West Tennessee Migratory Bird Conservation Area	TN	A, R, O	$50,000	$1,760,122	$1,810,122	6/20/2001
Total			**$4,100,000**	**$18,447,595**	**$22,547,595**	
Laguna Madre	TX	A, E, R, O	$993,694	$3,814,878	$4,808,572	9/10/2002
Magic Ridge Migratory Bird & Wetlands Sanctuary	TX	A, E	$50,000	$219,121	$269,121	6/12/2002
Playa Lakes WMA: Sediment Removal at Cattail Lake & Moist Soil Management	TX	E, R	$50,000	$76,391	$126,391	6/12/2002
Port Bolivar Wetlands Protection	TX	A, E, R, O	$450,000	$516,500	$966,500	3/14/2002
Wetlands Restoration Within the West Gulf Coastal Plain	TX	R	$467,500	$1,380,640	$1,848,140	9/21/2001
Total			**$2,011,194**	**$6,007,530**	**$8,018,724**	
Control of Phragmites at Ambassador Duck Club	UT	R	$37,000	$45,689	$82,689	6/20/2001
Utah Lake Wetlands	UT	A, R, O	$1,000,000	$3,357,891	$4,357,891	9/10/2002
Total			**$1,037,000**	**$3,403,580**	**$4,440,580**	
Cedar Island Conservation Initiative	VA	A	$50,000	$88,859	$138,859	6/20/2001
Chesapeake Bay Initiative II	VA, DE, MD, PA, WV	R	$533,000	$1,532,628	$2,065,628	6/12/2002
Chesapeake Bay Initiative III	VA, DE, MD, PA, WV	R	$1,000,000	$2,006,410	$3,006,410	9/10/2002
Lackey Farm Restoration & Conservation Project	VA	A, R, O	$49,620	$65,618	$115,238	6/12/2002
Roanoke River Migratory Bird Initiative I	VA, NC	A, E, R, O	$965,339	$2,706,924	$3,672,263	3/19/2003
Sound Investment I	VA, NC	A, E, R, O	$1,000,000	$2,354,991	$3,354,991	3/19/2003
Southeast Virginia Watersheds Project II	VA	A, R	$502,974	$2,411,528	$2,914,502	9/21/2001
Whitehurst Marsh Acquisition II	VA	A, E, R, O	$1,000,000	$4,368,079	$5,368,079	3/14/2002
Total			**$5,100,933**	**$15,535,037**	**$20,635,970**	

Multistate projects are listed in each state where they occur. Full figures are given with each listing.

U.S. North American Wetlands Conservation Act Projects Arrayed by State
Federal and Partner Dollars Invested in Fiscal Years 2002-2003
[Section 10(2)]

Project Title	State	Project Type	Grant Amount	Partner Amount	Total Amount	Date Approved
Connecticut River: Northern Valley Conservation	VT, NH	A, O	$914,000	$12,757,000	$13,671,000	3/14/2002
Total			$914,000	$12,757,000	$13,671,000	
Acquisition & Restoration of Misner Woods	WA	A, R	$50,000	$1,335,300	$1,385,300	6/12/2002
Bell Creek Wetland Prairie Restoration Project	WA	R	$49,990	$60,535	$110,525	6/12/2002
Channeled Scablands Focus Area I	WA	A, E, R, O	$978,641	$5,270,590	$6,249,231	9/21/2001
Christensen Pond Bird Sanctuary	WA	A	$47,200	$422,800	$470,000	6/20/2001
Columbia River Estuary Project	WA, OR	A, E, R, O	$997,000	$7,653,553	$8,650,553	3/14/2002
Crow Marsh Project	WA	A	$50,000	$345,000	$395,000	6/20/2001
Green Cove Basin Wetlands Protection Project	WA	A, O	$50,000	$100,000	$150,000	6/20/2001
Hines Marsh Restoration II	WA	A, E, R	$50,000	$96,008	$146,008	6/20/2001
Skagit/Samish Priority Wetlands Habitat Protection & Restoration II	WA	A, R, O	$922,068	$2,026,844	$2,948,912	3/14/2002
Snohomish Wetlands I	WA	A, R, O	$1,000,000	$6,828,566	$7,828,566	3/19/2003
South Shore Grays Harbor Project	WA	A, R	$955,000	$2,048,800	$3,003,800	9/21/2001
The Port Susan Bay All Bird Initiative	WA	A, E, R	$955,000	$995,000	$1,950,000	9/21/2001
West Hylebos Salmon Acquisition Project	WA	A	$50,000	$259,000	$309,000	6/20/2001
Willapa Bay II	WA	A, R	$986,792	$2,481,181	$3,467,973	9/10/2002
Total			$7,141,691	$29,923,177	$37,064,868	
Glacial Habitat Restoration Area IV	WI	A, E, R, O	$1,000,000	$2,133,280	$3,133,280	3/14/2002
Leland Marsh/Baraboo Range Conservation Easement Project	WI	A	$50,000	$54,604	$104,604	6/12/2002
Lower Chippewa River Wetland Protection Partnership	WI	A, R, O	$1,000,000	$2,289,800	$3,289,800	9/10/2002
Scuppernong River Wetland Restoration	WI	A, R	$50,000	$111,000	$161,000	6/12/2002
South-Central Wisconsin Prairie Pothole Initiative II	WI	A, E, R, O	$1,000,000	$2,440,187	$3,440,187	3/19/2003
Southeast Wisconsin Coastal Habitat Initiative III	WI	A, E, R, O	$995,638	$2,112,949	$3,108,587	9/21/2001
Superior Coastal Wetland Initiative II	WI	A, E, R, O	$999,800	$2,212,948	$3,212,748	9/10/2002
Wisconsin Waterfowl Association Shallow Wetland	WI	R	$50,000	$50,000	$100,000	6/20/2001
Total			$5,145,438	$11,404,768	$16,550,206	
Chesapeake Bay Initiative II	WV, DE, MD, PA, VA	R	$533,000	$1,532,628	$2,065,628	6/12/2002
Chesapeake Bay Initiative III	WV, DE, MD, PA, VA	R	$1,000,000	$2,006,410	$3,006,410	9/10/2002
Total			$1,533,000	$3,539,038	$5,072,038	
Clive Ostenberg Flyway Project	WY, NE	A	$50,000	$250,000	$300,000	6/20/2001
Lower Green River Wetland Restoration Project	WY	R	$49,072	$177,392	$226,464	6/20/2001
Teton River Basin Wetlands Conservation III	WY, ID	A, R, O	$1,000,000	$5,415,098	$6,415,098	9/10/2002
Total			$1,099,072	$5,842,490	$6,941,562	

Multistate projects are listed in each state where they occur. Full figures are given with each listing.

Canadian North American Wetlands Conservation Act Projects Arrayed by Province
Federal and Partner Dollars Invested in Fiscal Years 2002-2003
[Section 10(2)]

Project Title	Province	Project Type	Grant Amount	Partner Amount	Total Amount	Date Approved
Alberta Critical Wetland & Upland Habitat	AB	A, E	$632,306	$1,053,843	$1,686,149	6/12/2002
Alberta Critical Wetland & Upland Habitat	AB	A, E	$687,500	$1,254,688	$1,942,188	6/25/2003
Alberta Habitat Program	AB	A, E	$4,140,125	$4,797,375	$8,937,500	6/25/2003
Alberta Habitat Program	AB, BC	A, E	$3,191,250	$3,770,850	$6,962,100	9/21/2001
Alberta Habitat Program	AB, BC	A, E	$2,949,750	$3,414,150	$6,363,900	6/12/2002
Alberta Habitat Program	AB, BC	A, E	$2,049,280	$2,421,760	$4,471,040	9/10/2002
Western Boreal Forest Program	AB, BC, MB, NT, NU, SK, YT	A, E	$3,000,000	$5,326,050	$8,326,050	6/12/2002
Western Boreal Forest Program	AB, BC, MB, NT, SK, YT	A	$1,064,938	$1,752,438	$2,817,376	6/25/2003
Total			**$17,715,149**	**$23,791,154**	**$41,506,303**	
Alberta Habitat Program	BC, AB	A, E	$3,191,250	$3,770,850	$6,962,100	9/21/2001
Alberta Habitat Program	BC, AB	A, E	$2,949,750	$3,414,150	$6,363,900	6/12/2002
Alberta Habitat Program	BC, AB	A, E	$2,049,280	$2,421,760	$4,471,040	9/10/2002
Coastal & Intermountain British Columbia	BC	A, E	$690,916	$1,365,916	$2,056,832	6/12/2002
Conservation of Critical Wetlands & Associated Upland Habitats, Coastal	BC	A, E	$689,294	$1,308,044	$1,997,338	6/25/2003
Conservation of Wetlands & Associated Upland Habitats, Coastal & Intermountain	BC	A, E	$621,690	$828,690	$1,450,380	9/21/2001
Conservation of Wetlands & Associated Upland Habitats, Coastal	BC	A, E	$399,360	$975,360	$1,374,720	9/10/2002
Critical British Columbia Coastal & Intermountain Wetland Habitats	BC	A, E	$375,000	$653,499	$1,028,499	6/25/2003
Critical British Columbia Coastal & Intermountain Wetland Habitats	BC	A, E	$912,241	$1,587,241	$2,499,482	6/12/2002
Critical Wetlands & Associated Upland Habitats, Intermountain	BC	A, E	$448,510	$792,260	$1,240,770	6/25/2003
South Okanagan Key Program Areas	BC	A, E	$200,100	$338,100	$538,200	9/21/2001
Western Boreal Forest Program	BC, AB, MB, NT, NU, SK, YT	A, E	$3,000,000	$5,326,050	$8,326,050	6/12/2002
Western Boreal Forest Program	BC, AB, MB, NT, SK, YT	A	$1,064,938	$1,752,438	$2,817,376	6/25/2003
Total			**$16,592,329**	**$24,534,358**	**$41,126,687**	
Manitoba Critical Upland & Wetland Habitat	MB	A, E, O	$658,125	$1,096,875	$1,755,000	6/12/2002
Manitoba Prairie Parkland Program	MB	A, E	$1,595,280	$1,636,680	$3,231,960	9/21/2001
Manitoba Prairie Parkland Program	MB	A, E	$1,251,450	$1,287,900	$2,539,350	6/12/2002
Manitoba Prairie Parkland Program	MB	A, E	$1,024,640	$1,065,600	$2,090,240	9/10/2002
Manitoba Prairie Parkland Program	MB	A, E	$1,851,438	$1,895,438	$3,746,876	6/25/2003
Potholes Plus Project	MB	A, E	$425,925	$618,300	$1,044,225	6/12/2002
Potholes Plus Project	MB	A, O	$592,625	$926,063	$1,518,688	6/25/2003
Western Boreal Forest Program	MB, AB, BC, NT, NU, SK, YT	A, E	$3,000,000	$5,326,050	$8,326,050	6/12/2002
Western Boreal Forest Program	MB, AB, BC, NT, SK, YT	A	$1,064,938	$1,752,438	$2,817,376	6/25/2003
Total			**$11,464,421**	**$15,605,344**	**$27,069,765**	

Multistate projects are listed in each state where they occur. Full figures are given with each listing.

Canadian North American Wetlands Conservation Act Projects Arrayed by Province
Federal and Partner Dollars Invested in Fiscal Years 2002-2003
[Section 10(2)]

Project Title	Province	Project Type	Grant Amount	Partner Amount	Total Amount	Date Approved
Bay of Fundy Habitat Securement Project	NB, NS	A	$199,800	$332,775	$532,575	6/12/2002
New Brunswick Wetlands	NB	A, E	$175,950	$300,150	$476,100	9/21/2001
New Brunswick Wetlands Conservation	NB	A, E	$172,125	$301,050	$473,175	6/12/2002
New Brunswick Wetlands Conservation	NB	A, E	$113,280	$202,880	$316,160	9/10/2002
New Brunswick Wetlands Conservation	NB	A, E	$253,859	$421,608	$675,467	6/25/2003
Northumberland Strait Coastal Wetland Securement	NB, NS, PEI	A	$199,994	$356,057	$556,051	6/25/2003
Total			**$1,115,008**	**$1,914,520**	**$3,029,528**	
Newfoundland & Labrador Coastal & Inland Freshwater Wetlands	NF	A, E	$56,580	$94,530	$151,110	9/21/2001
Newfoundland & Labrador Coastal & Inland Freshwater Wetlands	NF	A, E	$51,300	$96,525	$147,825	6/12/2002
Newfoundland & Labrador Coastal & Inland Freshwater Wetlands	NF	A, E	$33,920	$65,920	$99,840	9/10/2002
Newfoundland & Labrador Coastal & Inland Freshwater Wetlands	NF	A, E	$68,750	$116,876	$185,626	6/25/2003
Total			**$210,550**	**$373,851**	**$584,401**	
Bay of Fundy Habitat Securement Project	NS, NB	A	$199,800	$332,775	$532,575	6/12/2002
Northumberland Strait Coastal Wetland Securement	NS, NB, PEI	A	$199,994	$356,057	$556,051	6/25/2003
Nova Scotia Coastal & Inland Wetlands	NS	A, E	$127,650	$212,520	$340,170	9/21/2001
Nova Scotia Coastal & Inland Wetlands	NS	A, E	$120,825	$221,400	$342,225	6/12/2002
Nova Scotia Coastal & Inland Wetlands	NS	A, E	$79,360	$179,840	$259,200	9/10/2002
Nova Scotia Coastal & Inland Wetlands	NS	A, E	$184,697	$311,197	$495,894	6/25/2003
Total			**$912,326**	**$1,613,789**	**$2,526,115**	
Western Boreal Forest Program	NT, AB, BC, MB, NU, SK, YT	A, E	$3,000,000	$5,326,050	$8,326,050	6/12/2002
Western Boreal Forest Program	NT, AB, BC, MB, SK, YT	A	$1,064,938	$1,752,438	$2,817,376	6/25/2003
Total			**$4,064,938**	**$7,078,488**	**$11,143,426**	
Western Boreal Forest Program	NU, AB, BC, MB, NT, SK, YT	A, E	$3,000,000	$5,326,050	$8,326,050	6/12/2002
Total			**$3,000,000**	**$5,326,050**	**$8,326,050**	
Great Lakes Wetland Habitat Project	ON	A, E	$199,375	$388,437	$587,812	6/25/2003
Ontario Regional Project	ON	A, E	$742,440	$1,237,170	$1,979,610	9/21/2001
Ontario Regional Project	ON	A, E	$899,775	$1,514,025	$2,413,800	6/12/2002
Ontario Regional Project	ON	A, E	$437,760	$732,160	$1,169,920	9/10/2002
Ontario Regional Project	ON	A, E	$1,268,094	$2,144,656	$3,412,750	6/25/2003
Ontario Wetland Habitat Conservation Project	ON	A, O	$337,500	$562,342	$899,842	6/12/2002
Ontario Wetland Habitat Fund Program	ON	A, E	$138,000	$471,891	$609,891	9/21/2001
Ontario Wetland Habitat Fund Program	ON	A, E	$128,000	$497,280	$625,280	9/10/2002
Total			**$4,150,944**	**$7,547,961**	**$11,698,905**	

Multistate projects are listed in each state where they occur. Full figures are given with each listing.

Canadian North American Wetlands Conservation Act Projects Arrayed by Province
Federal and Partner Dollars Invested in Fiscal Years 2002-2003
[Section 10(2)]

Project Title	Province	Project Type	Grant Amount	Partner Amount	Total Amount	Date Approved
Northumberland Strait Coastal Wetland Securement	PEI, NB, NS	A	$199,994	$356,057	$556,051	6/25/2003
Prince Edward Island Wetlands in the Agricultural Landscape	PEI	A, E	$88,320	$243,570	$331,890	9/21/2001
Prince Edward Island Wetlands in the Agricultural Landscape	PEI	A, E	$105,975	$204,525	$310,500	6/12/2002
Prince Edward Island Wetlands in the Agricultural Landscape	PEI	A, E	$56,320	$145,920	$202,240	9/10/2002
Prince Edward Island Wetlands in the Agricultural Landscape	PEI	A, E	$139,356	$254,858	$394,214	6/25/2003
Total			$589,965	$1,204,930	$1,794,895	
Quebec/St. Lawrence & Adjoining Landscapes	QC	A, E	$440,220	$810,750	$1,250,970	9/21/2001
Quebec/St. Lawrence & Adjoining Landscapes	QC	A, E	$449,550	$759,375	$1,208,925	6/12/2002
Quebec/St. Lawrence & Adjoining Landscapes	QC	A, E	$282,880	$535,680	$818,560	9/10/2002
Quebec/St. Lawrence & Adjoining Landscapes	QC	A, E	$646,594	$1,346,469	$1,993,063	6/25/2003
Quebec Critical Wetland & Upland Habitat	QC	A, E, O	$100,000	$381,250	$481,250	6/25/2003
Total			$1,919,244	$3,833,524	$5,752,768	
Saskatchewan Critical Wetland & Upland Habitat	SK	A, E	$632,800	$1,054,700	$1,687,500	6/12/2002
Saskatchewan Habitat Program	SK	A, E	$3,121,560	$3,345,810	$6,467,370	9/21/2001
Saskatchewan Habitat Program	SK	A, E	$2,949,750	$3,165,750	$6,115,500	6/12/2002
Saskatchewan Habitat Program	SK	A, E	$1,964,160	$2,172,160	$4,136,320	9/10/2002
Saskatchewan Habitat Program	SK	A, E	$4,140,125	$4,360,125	$8,500,250	6/25/2003
Saskatchewan Prairie Shores Project	SK	A, R	$69,000	$207,000	$276,000	9/21/2001
Saskatchewan Prairie Shores Project	SK	A, E	$84,800	$277,000	$361,800	9/10/2002
Western Boreal Forest Program	SK, AB, BC, MB, NT, NU, YT	A, E	$3,000,000	$5,326,050	$8,326,050	6/12/2002
Western Boreal Forest Program	SK, AB, BC, MB, NT, YT	A	$1,064,938	$1,752,438	$2,817,376	6/25/2003
Total			$17,027,133	$21,661,033	$38,688,166	
Western Boreal Forest Program	YT, AB, BC, MB, NT, NU, SK	A, E	$3,000,000	$5,326,050	$8,326,050	6/12/2002
Western Boreal Forest Program	YT, AB, BC, MB, NT, SK	A	$1,064,938	$1,752,438	$2,817,376	6/25/2003
Total			$4,064,938	$7,078,488	$11,143,426	

Multistate projects are listed in each state where they occur. Full figures are given with each listing.

Mexican North American Wetlands Conservation Act Projects Arrayed by State
Federal and Partner Dollars Invested in Fiscal Years 2002-2003
[Section 10(2)]

Project Title	State	Project Type	Grant Amount	Partner Amount	Total Amount	Date Approved
A Community Partnership - Rio Hardy in the Colorado River Delta	BCN	R, O	$63,800	$63,850	$127,650	6/12/2002
Conservation & Sustainable Use of Wetlands, La Asamblea - San Francisquito Coastal	BCN	O	$146,230	$214,020	$360,250	3/19/2003
Monitoring & Outreach Plan for the Upper Gulf of California & Colorado River Delta	BCN, SON	O	$134,842	$137,597	$272,439	3/19/2003
Regionalization of the Pie, Coastal Wetlands in Northwest Mexico	BCN, BCS, NAY, SIN	O	$149,132	$236,800	$385,932	9/21/2001
Total			**$494,004**	**$652,267**	**$1,146,271**	
Protection of Wetlands, Reefs, & Birds in the Revillagigedo Archipelago II	BCS	O	$184,000	$184,000	$368,000	9/10/2002
Regionalization of the Pie, Coastal Wetlands in Northwest Mexico	BCS, BCN, NAY, SIN	O	$149,132	$236,800	$385,932	9/21/2001
Total			**$333,132**	**$420,800**	**$753,932**	
Training in the Management of & Response to Health Contingencies of Waterfowl	CHIH, DF, YUC	O	$109,520	$122,250	$231,770	3/19/2003
Wetlands of Importance for the Arctic Goose II	CHIH, COAH, DGO, NL, TAMPS, ZAC	O	$77,830	$90,713	$168,543	3/14/2002
Total			**$187,350**	**$212,963**	**$400,313**	
Conservation of Priority Wetlands in Chiapas	CHIS	O	$332,176	$332,380	$664,556	3/19/2003
Environmental Status Evaluation, Playas De Catazaja Phase II	CHIS, TAB	O	$89,868	$105,978	$195,846	3/14/2002
Inventory & Classification of Critical Wetlands in Mexico	CHIS, GRO, OAX	O	$244,537	$298,289	$542,826	3/19/2003
The 2002 Veracruz Model	CHIS	O	$67,500	$114,675	$182,175	3/14/2002
Wetlands Conservation Corridor, Pacific Coastal Plain of Chiapas - Oaxaca	CHIS, OAX	O	$192,392	$199,537	$391,929	9/21/2001
Total			**$926,473**	**$1,050,859**	**$1,977,332**	
Wetlands of Importance for the Arctic Goose II	COAH, CHIH, DGO, NL, TAMPS, ZAC	O	$77,830	$90,713	$168,543	3/14/2002
Total			**$77,830**	**$90,713**	**$168,543**	
Training in the Management of & Response to Health Contingencies of Waterfowl	DF, CHIH, YUC	O	$109,520	$122,250	$231,770	3/19/2003
Total			**$109,520**	**$122,250**	**$231,770**	
Durangueno Wetlands	DGO	E	$226,100	$478,435	$704,535	6/12/2002
Wetlands of Importance for the Arctic Goose II	DGO, CHIH, COAH, NL, TAMPS, ZAC	O	$77,830	$90,713	$168,543	3/14/2002
Total			**$303,930**	**$569,148**	**$873,078**	

Multistate projects are listed in each state where they occur. Full figures are given with each listing.

Mexican North American Wetlands Conservation Act Projects Arrayed by State
Federal and Partner Dollars Invested in Fiscal Years 2002-2003
[Section 10(2)]

Project Title	State	Project Type	Grant Amount	Partner Amount	Total Amount	Date Approved
Inventory & Classification of Critical Wetlands in Mexico	GRO, CHIS, OAX	O	$244,537	$298,289	$542,826	3/19/2003
Total			$244,537	$298,289	$542,826	
Rio Laja Wetlands Protection Project II	GTO	R, O	$219,215	$521,165	$740,380	9/10/2002
Rivers Restoration of Five Microwatersheds of La Purisima Watershed	GTO	R, O	$162,515	$197,848	$360,364	9/10/2002
Total			$381,730	$719,013	$1,100,744	
Regionalization of the Pie, Coastal Wetlands in Northwest Mexico	NAY, BCN, BCS, SIN	O	$149,132	$236,800	$385,932	9/21/2001
Total			$149,132	$236,800	$385,932	
National Strategy for the Conservation of Waterfowl & Their Habitats	NL	O	$40,675	$52,500	$93,175	3/19/2003
National Strategy for the Conservation of Shorebirds & Their Habitats	NL, SIN	O	$55,905	$57,989	$113,894	3/19/2003
Wetlands of Importance for the Arctic Goose II	NL, CHIH, COAH, DGO, TAMPS, ZAC	O	$77,830	$90,713	$168,543	3/14/2002
Total			$174,410	$201,202	$375,612	
Inventory & Classification of Critical Wetlands in Mexico	OAX, CHIS, GRO	O	$244,537	$298,289	$542,826	3/19/2003
Wetlands Conservation Corridor, Pacific Coastal Plain of Chiapas - Oaxaca	OAX, CHIS	O	$192,392	$199,537	$391,929	9/21/2001
Total			$436,929	$497,826	$934,755	
Conservation of Banco Chinchorro Biosphere Reserve Wetlands II	QROO	O	$159,104	$171,245	$330,349	9/10/2002
Establishment of Management, Monitoring, Visitor Center, & Acquisition of Pez Maya	QROO	A	$400,000	$2,746,000	$3,146,000	9/21/2001
Total			$559,104	$2,917,245	$3,476,349	
Conserving Bird Habitats in Western Mexico III	SIN	O	$140,251	$310,995	$451,246	3/19/2003
Ensenada De Pabellones	SIN	O	$136,522	$269,350	$405,872	3/14/2002
National Strategy for the Conservation of Shorebirds and Their Habitats	SIN, NL	O	$55,905	$57,989	$113,894	3/19/2003
Regionalization of the Pie, Coastal Wetlands in Northwest Mexico	SIN, BCN, BCS, NAY	O	$149,132	$236,800	$385,932	9/21/2001
Total			$481,810	$875,134	$1,356,944	
Management Strategies for Restoration of the Colorado River Delta Floodplain	SON	O	$239,759	$248,000	$487,759	3/19/2003
Monitoring & Outreach Plan for the Upper Gulf of California & Colorado River Delta	SON, BCN	O	$134,842	$137,597	$272,439	3/19/2003
Restoration of Cienega De San Bernardino Watershed, Phase II	SON	A, R	$369,574	$500,000	$869,574	3/14/2002
Total			$744,175	$885,597	$1,629,772	

Multistate projects are listed in each state where they occur. Full figures are given with each listing.

Mexican North American Wetlands Conservation Act Projects Arrayed by State
Federal and Partner Dollars in Fiscal Years Invested 2002-2003
[Section 10(2)]

Project Title	State	Project Type	Grant Amount	Partner Amount	Total Amount	Date Approved
Environmental Status Evaluation, Playas De Catazaja Phase II	TAB, CHIS	O	$89,868	$105,978	$195,846	3/14/2002
Participatory Research & Environmental Education, El Rosario Lagoon	TAB	O	$119,166	$120,690	$239,856	3/19/2003
Total			**$209,034**	**$226,668**	**$435,702**	
Rancho El Hermalbo	TAMPS	E, O	$56,707	$74,026	$130,733	3/14/2002
Rehabilitation of the Anda la Piedra Lagoon, Laguna Madre	TAMPS	R, O	$155,780	$175,780	$331,560	9/10/2002
Wetlands of Importance for the Arctic Goose II	TAMPS, NL, CHIH, COAH, DGO, ZAC	O	$77,830	$90,713	$168,543	3/14/2002
Total			**$290,317**	**$340,519**	**$630,836**	
Conservation & Management of the Wetlands of Alvarado	VER	O	$339,180	$430,960	$770,140	6/12/2002
Development of a Model for Citizen Participation, Management/Restoration	VER	O	$119,100	$187,367	$306,467	9/21/2001
Establishment of an Environmental Management Unit, Alvarado Wetland	VER	O	$192,668	$712,348	$905,016	6/12/2002
Planning, Municipal Ecological Policies & Resource Development, Tuxpan	VER	O	$49,650	$51,091	$100,741	9/21/2001
Total			**$700,598**	**$1,381,766**	**$2,082,364**	
La Microcuenca Costera de Chabihau	YUC	R, O	$73,881	$80,731	$154,612	9/10/2002
Purchase of Land Rights, Birds & Wildlife Habitat	YUC	A, O	$249,300	$258,006	$507,306	9/21/2001
Restoration, Dzilam State Reserve, Ria Lagartos Biosphere Reserve III	YUC	E, O	$116,226	$181,818	$298,044	9/10/2002
Restauracion de Cobertura Vegetal, El Palmar II	YUC	R	$153,543	$155,000	$308,543	9/21/2001
San Crisanto, a Sustainable Development II	YUC	R	$68,208	$68,411	$136,619	3/14/2002
Training in the Management of & Response to Health Contingencies of Waterfowl	YUC, CHIH, DF	O	$109,520	$122,250	$231,770	3/19/2003
Total			**$770,678**	**$866,216**	**$1,636,894**	
Wetlands of Importance for the Arctic Goose II	ZAC, CHIH, COAH, DGO, NL, TAMPS	O	$77,830	$90,713	$168,543	3/14/2002
Total			**$77,830**	**$90,713**	**$168,543**	

Multistate projects are listed in each state where they occur. Full figures are given with each listing.

North American Wetlands Conservation Act
The North American Wetlands Conservation Council

Duane Shroufe (Chair), Director, Arizona Game and Fish Department

Steve Williams, Director, U.S. Fish and Wildlife Service

John Cooper, Secretary, South Dakota Department of Game, Fish and Parks

John Berry, Executive Secretary, National Fish and Wildlife Foundation

Michael Dennis, Vice President and General Counsel, The Nature Conservancy

KiKu Hoagland Hanes, Board of Directors Member, The Conservation Fund

Wayne MacCallum, Director, Massachusetts Division of Fisheries and Wildlife

Steve Miller, Administrator of Land Division, Wisconsin Department of Natural Resources

Alan Wentz, Group Manager for Conservation Programs, Ducks Unlimited, Inc.

David Nomsen (Alternate), Director of Governmental Affairs, Pheasants Forever, Inc.

Mary Hope Hutson (Ex Officio), Vice President, The Land Trust Alliance

Georgita Ruiz (Ex Officio), Director General de Vida Silvestre, SEMARNAT

Karen Brown (Ex Officio), Assistant Deputy Minister, Environment Canada

David Smith (Council Coordinator), Chief, Division of Bird Habitat Conservation,
U.S. Fish and Wildlife Service

recommends projects for funding to
The Migratory Bird Conservation Commission

Honorable Gale Norton (Chair), Secretary of the Interior

Honorable John Breaux, Senator from Louisiana

Honorable Thad Cochran, Senator from Mississippi

Honorable, John Dingell, Representative from Michigan

Honorable Curt Weldon, Representative from Pennsylvania

Honorable Mike Leavitt, Environmental Protection Agency Administrator

Honorable Dan Glickman, Secretary of Agriculture

Mr. Eric Alvarez (Secretary), Chief, Division of Realty,
U.S. Fish and Wildlife Service

The names listed above reflect current membership.

". . . to conserve North American wetland ecosystems and waterfowl and the other migratory birds and fish and wildlife that depend upon such habitats."

NORTH AMERICAN WETLANDS CONSERVATION ACT

North American Wetlands Conservation Council

NORTH AMERICAN WETLANDS CONSERVATION COUNCIL
4401 N. FAIRFAX DRIVE, MAILSTOP 4075
ARLINGTON, VIRGINIA 22203
PH: 703-358-1784
FAX: 703-358-2282

Printed on recycled paper

www.ingramcontent.com/pod-product-compliance
Lightning Source LLC
Chambersburg PA
CBHW080622290526

45790CB00007B/2892